Mentoring and Coaching in Schools

Can mentoring and coaching really improve professional practice? How can research and inquiry improve mentoring and coaching practice?

Mentoring and Coaching in Schools explores the ways in which mentoring and coaching can be used as a dynamic collaborative process for effective professional learning. It demonstrates how the use of practitioner inquiry within mentoring and coaching relationships in schools results in professional learning which is both transformative and empowering for teachers.

The book sets out a new model for mentoring and coaching which is centred on a process of critical inquiry and shows teachers how they can use this model to carry out their own collaborative inquiries. Features include:

- reflective questions, guidelines, tasks and templates to help collect evidence and evaluate inquiries;
- detailed case studies focusing on teachers at different stages in their career;
- practical guidance on carrying out practitioner inquiry and research;
- an analysis of learning outcomes resulting from different coaching and mentoring relationships.

This timely text will be valuable reading for coaches and mentors in secondary schools, teachers undertaking continuing professional development and students on coaching and mentoring courses.

Suzanne Burley is Academic Leader for Teacher Education and Professional Learning at London Metropolitan University.

Cathy Pomphrey was Academic Leader for Initial Teacher Education at London Metropolitan University and now works as an education consultant.

Mentoring and Coaching in Schools

Professional learning through collaborative inquiry

Suzanne Burley and
Cathy Pomphrey

Routledge
Taylor & Francis Group

LONDON AND NEW YORK

This first edition published 2011
by Routledge
2 Park Square, Milton Park, Abingdon, Oxon OX14 4RN

Simultaneously published in the USA and Canada
by Routledge
711 Third Avenue, New York, NY 10017

Routledge is an imprint of the Taylor & Francis Group, an informa business

© 2011 Suzanne Burley and Cathy Pomphrey

British Library Cataloguing in Publication Data
A catalogue record for this book is available from the British Library

Library of Congress Cataloging-in-Publication Data
Burley, Suzanne.
Mentoring and coaching in schools: professional learning through collaborative inquiry / by Suzanne Burley and Cathy Pomphrey.—1st ed.
    p. cm.
Includes bibliographical references and index.
1. Mentoring in education—United States. 2. Teaching teams—United States. 3. Teachers—In-service training—United States. I. Pomphrey, Cathy. II. Title.
LB1731.4.B87 2011
371.102—dc22   2010041813

ISBN13: 978-0-415-56361-1 (hbk)
ISBN13: 978-0-415-56363-5 (pbk)
ISBN13: 978-0-203-82182-4 (ebk)

Typeset in Sabon
by Book Now Ltd, London
Printed and bound in Great Britain by
TJ International Ltd, Padstow, Cornwall

Contents

Illustrations

Evaluation templates

Tables

Acknowledgements

The authors wish to thank all those who have contributed to the case studies within this book and the teachers and tutors who have participated in the postgraduate certificate in mentoring and coaching in schools course at London Metropolitan University. Special thanks are due to:

Maggi Fisher
Viv Grant
Sol Ibrahim
Alex Josephy
Teddy Prout

Introduction

This book provides a new perspective on mentoring and coaching in secondary schools. It explores the ways in which mentoring and coaching can be used as a dynamic process for effective professional learning in order to bring about change in professional practice. It shows how mentoring and coaching can make use of collaborative practitioner inquiry to develop effective professional learning in order to bring about this change in professional practice.

The book is the result of a collaboration between university academics and school professionals and arises directly from the development of a postgraduate certificate in 'Mentoring and Coaching in Schools' developed and taught by the authors. The authors have an in-depth knowledge and experience of the work of schools and higher education institutions. Both have extensive experience of providing teacher education and professional development at all levels. The authors have a long tradition of collaboration in researching, teaching and writing. They have delivered professional development courses at both national and international levels.

The audience for this book is primarily secondary school teachers, although all education professionals in both national and international contexts will find many ideas of relevance to them. It can be used by all teachers engaged in professional learning at various stages in their careers, for example in trainee teacher mentoring and/or coaching relationships, teachers undertaking postgraduate courses such as the Masters in Teaching and Learning (MTL) or those preparing for leadership roles.

Teachers are now expected to take increasing responsibility for their own professional learning and development and this book will support collaborative professional learning for teachers through mentoring and coaching relationships at different stages of their career. Mentoring and coaching processes are widely used in schools, and this book demonstrates innovative ways of using and developing these processes in order to achieve transformative professional learning.

The book introduces theoretical discussion about professional learning, mentoring and coaching and practitioner inquiry in order to provide a conceptual framework to underpin authentic examples of recent inquiry-based collaborative professional practice focused on mentoring and coaching. These examples of inquiry-based collaborative professional practice focus on teachers at different stages of their career and also provide comparisons with mentoring and coaching practice in other professions. Throughout the book, teachers are supported in the development of their professional learning by a series of tasks which consolidate their reading and give detailed guidance for completing their own inquiries related to mentoring and coaching practice.

There is a wealth of literature which addresses mentoring and coaching from both theoretical and practical perspectives. The current policy context in much of Britain, which increasingly advocates an extensive use of mentoring and/or coaching processes as an important part of individual and institutional professional learning and development, has contributed to the creation of many of these texts. Some of these texts are examined in this book. There is also now an increasing professionalisation of mentoring and coaching in education and consequently a need to re-examine the key concepts and practices which inform the relationship between mentoring and coaching and professional learning practices. This re-examination is the intention of this book.

What is new about the ideas presented in this book is the ways in which links are made between mentoring and coaching, professional learning and critical inquiry. These ideas show how transformative professional learning can be achieved through using critical inquiry as a key process for examining and practising mentoring and coaching. The book uses an important concept derived from the work of Wenger (1998) on communities of practice and used by Ponte (2010) and Smith (2000) to conceptualise a metaphorical space in which the mentoring and coaching relationship becomes a learning platform.

This platform is a space where dialogue and professional learning can be achieved through collaborative critical inquiry. It is also a space where teachers can develop a shared focus and purpose for their professional learning. The mentoring and coaching learning platform provides the space to create a collaborative approach to focused and purposeful critical inquiry. Engagement in critical inquiry provides a clear focus and direction for the mentoring and coaching collaboration. As DuFour *et al.* (2006) state: 'The fact that teachers collaborate will do nothing to improve a school. The pertinent question is not, "Are they collaborating?" but rather, "What are they collaborating about?"' (p. 113).

The critical inquiry process needs to be informed by evidence as proposed by Lingard and Renshaw (2010: 26–39) as analysing evidence allows teachers to use professional judgement in evaluating professional practice and learning. In Chapter 1, teachers are given guidelines on ways of documenting and analysing the evidence they have gathered as a result of engaging with the issues presented in this book. The critical inquiry approach is also used to examine issues about mentoring and coaching from different professional contexts to provide comparative analysis between practice in schools and other contexts.

The book is organised in two parts. Part I provides theoretical discussions of professional learning, mentoring and coaching and collaborative practitioner inquiry and explores the links between all these areas. It starts by providing practical guidance for teachers on using the book to support their reading, reflection and development of professional learning inquiries. Part II documents a range of teacher inquiries which examine the inter-relationship between mentoring and coaching, practitioner-based inquiry and collaborative professional learning and offer insights into a variety of mentoring and coaching roles and contexts. Each chapter in Part II examines a different type of mentoring and coaching collaboration and the inquiries included in these chapters are provided by educational practitioners most of whom are teachers. The book ends with a conclusion which links the common threads and provides a way forward offering a new perspective on mentoring and coaching.

Part I

Chapter 1, 'Using this book to develop professional learning through mentoring and coaching', develops the evidence base for individuals to reflect on their professional learning. **This chapter should be read before reading the rest of the book.** It provides evaluation templates to support teachers' reflections on academic reading and the development and evaluation of critical inquiries.

Chapter 2, 'Dimensions of professional learning', examines definitions and understandings of the different types of learning which constitute professional learning. It considers the purposes, nature and achievement of professional learning and links this to mentoring and coaching and critical inquiry. Chapter 3, 'Mentoring and coaching: a platform for professional learning', examines a number of theoretical and policy models of mentoring and coaching and explores current definitions related to these. It traces and critiques the development and use of mentoring and coaching for professional learning in schools and proposes an alternative set of principles to guide the development of mentoring and coaching in a school context. Chapter 4, 'Practitioner inquiry for professional learning in mentoring and coaching', explores and introduces the term 'practitioner inquiry', linking it with professional learning and mentoring and coaching. It offers a model which shows how critical inquiries can be carried out at a number of levels. This is shown as the 'practitioner inquiry spectrum'.

Part II

Chapter 5, 'Inquiring into the nature of mentoring and coaching through collaboration', explores mentoring and coaching in secondary schools by examining the outcomes of collaboration between and by teacher participants taking a postgraduate course on mentoring and coaching in schools. It discusses the nature and quality of the different collaborations throughout the course and shows how taking a critical inquiry-based approach within these collaborations led to transformative professional learning related to mentoring and coaching.

Chapters 6 to 8 contain a range of critical collaborative inquiries undertaken by secondary school teachers and other education professionals which investigate different mentoring and coaching relationships. Chapter 6, 'Inquiring into mentoring and coaching in a range of professional contexts', identifies what schools can learn from the outcomes of inquiries into different understandings and uses of mentoring and coaching in a range of professional contexts. Chapter 7, 'Inquiring into one-to-one mentoring and coaching collaborations within the school context', shows the outcomes of inquiries into one-to-one mentoring and coaching collaborations where the inquirers are at the same time participating in the collaboration while also conducting the inquiry. This chapter illustrates the reciprocal learning which took place within mentoring and coaching collaborations between teachers at different stages of their careers. Chapter 8, 'Inquiring into wider mentoring and coaching collaborations within the school context', shows the development of larger-scale inquiries which worked with groups and teams of school professionals to set up new systems and approaches for mentoring and/or coaching. This chapter demonstrates the potential of mentoring and coaching for effecting institutional change.

The concluding chapter, 'A new perspective: mentoring and coaching as collaborative professional inquiry', provides a new perspective on the processes of mentoring and coaching. It assesses the links between the mentoring and coaching inquiries presented in Part II and the theoretical ideas discussed in Part I. It argues for an approach to mentoring and coaching in secondary schools which recognises the potential of this collaborative relationship to develop criticality through the use of practitioner inquiry in order to achieve transformative professional learning.

1

Using this book to develop professional learning through mentoring and coaching

Key learning points

- how to reflect on and make use of academic reading;
- how to carry out inquiries into mentoring and coaching;
- how to evaluate inquiries for effective professional learning;
- undertaking tasks and inquiries related to each chapter.

This chapter enables teachers to employ the material in the book in order to use mentoring and coaching to develop their own professional learning in a practical and pro-active way. Mentoring and coaching provides the ideal opportunity for teachers to collaborate in a number of ways and productive collaboration is an essential aspect of institutional and individual professional learning.

The book is divided into two parts; the first part contains theoretical information about professional learning, mentoring and coaching and practitioner inquiry, while the second part provides case studies which illustrate how teachers have collaborated in using inquiries to develop their professional learning through mentoring and coaching.

This chapter aims to structure teachers' engagement with these two distinct parts of the book and can be used flexibly to support the professional learning which can be derived from each chapter. Teachers will be able to gather evidence of this professional learning through engaging with the guidance in this chapter.

Part I

Part I (Chapters 2, 3 and 4) covers the following areas:

- dimensions of professional learning;
- mentoring and coaching: a platform for professional learning;
- practitioner inquiry for professional learning in mentoring and coaching.

A series of reflective questions for teachers are provided below to support Part I. These will enable teachers to record, reflect on and analyse the potential for application of their reading.

Reflective questions for Part I

These reflective questions can be used after reading each chapter in Part I. The questions are divided into three areas.

1. Recording the key theoretical concepts presented in each chapter.
2. Reflecting on these concepts in relation to individual experience.
3. Analysing how these theoretical concepts make sense of professional experience and could inform the development of practice within a school context.

Recording

- Use the key learning points at the start of each chapter as subheadings to record the main ideas presented.
- Note the names of the main researchers or policy-makers who produced these ideas.

Reflecting

Examine the main ideas produced and consider them in relation to the following:

- ideas that have a resonance with current and previous personal professional knowledge, experience and practice;
- ideas that are new or question previously held values, beliefs and assumptions.

For ideas that resonate with current or previous professional knowledge, experience and practice, consider the following questions:

■ How did this idea originate?
■ Does the information in the chapter add to or change previous conceptions?

For ideas that are new or question previously held values, beliefs and assumptions:

■ What is the significance of the new idea?
■ How does it impact on current professional knowledge and understanding?

Analysing

Use the reflections above to identify the following:

■ ideas to explore further;
■ questions to ask in relation to individual and institutional professional practices;
■ possible ways to change or develop current professional practices; potential sources of support or barriers to change or development.

Part II

For Part II, guidelines are provided to support teachers in developing their own collaborative critical inquiries. These guidelines include suggested tasks, examples and tables to support inquiries. The evaluation templates included at the end of Chapter 1 give teachers the opportunity to evaluate the inquiries they have developed in order to both reflect on and progress their professional learning.

In this part an investigation is provided at the end of each chapter. These investigations are divided into three components:

1. *purpose,* which gives an aim for the inquiry to be carried out;
2. *action,* which sets out a process for the inquiry;

3. *evaluation,* which enables teachers to assess the effectiveness of the whole inquiry process.

It is the evaluation stage which ensures that teachers are able to make connections between processes and outcomes in their collaborative mentoring and coaching inquiries and can apply these to future professional learning.

The inquiry in each investigation can be evaluated using Evaluation Template 1.1 provided in the Appendix to this chapter. Additionally, teachers can analyse their inquiry using the practitioner inquiry spectrum discussed in Chapter 4 (pp. 49–52) and reproduced in the Appendix (Evaluation Template 1.2). Teachers can use this further evaluation template to consider where on the spectrum each aspect of their inquiry is situated.

Before undertaking the investigations linked to Part II, teachers may find completing the following task helpful in understanding the three key components of the investigation structure.

Task

Read the following account of a teacher's inquiry which was designed to introduce specialist coaching to develop skills for teaching assistants. Compare this account with the suggestions for evaluation given in Evaluation Templates 1.1 and 1.2 and identify ways in which using the templates might produce a more useful and incisive assessment of the inquiry, the professional learning achieved and the possibilities for future individual and institutional development.

Teachers will also find it useful to note any places in the account where it would be helpful to have more information and detail in order to be clearer about the purpose and process of the inquiry.

An inquiry into developing teaching assistants (TAs) within the school workforce

This inquiry looks at the question 'Can a mentoring or coaching process enhance the experience of teaching assistants in supporting arts based lessons?'.

Context

The school in the study is a large urban school with specialist arts status. The issue of TAs supporting in arts lessons arose when both the head of the learning support faculty and the head of the performing and visual arts faculty were discussing professional development. A number of TAs felt under-confident in supporting arts lessons as some of them had no experience or training in music, dance or art. It was agreed that the two heads of faculty would lead an initial professional development session to discuss what TAs wanted and what arts staff expected.

Process

The initial professional development session
This looked at the needs of the TAs in order to support the specific students they were responsible for, as well as being able to support the main teacher in delivering the curriculum to the class as a whole. There were two main issues that came out of this from a mentoring point of view. The first was that the TAs needed to be able to do certain things within the lesson to be able to support the students, the second was the lack of self-confidence that the TAs expressed in order to support properly.

Further professional development sessions
A number of following sessions, run by the arts teachers, developed skills that the TAs said they were lacking. For example, the music department ran several sessions on the basics of playing the keyboard, guitar and drums, while the dance department ran several sessions on the basics of the waltz and tango steps. All the arts teachers looked specifically at raising the self-confidence of the TAs involved. They worked with individual TAs to find out what their main issue was, and tackled that, before addressing the wider issues that would allow the best possible support for the teacher in the classroom.

Outcomes

1. confidence of TAs in arts lessons;
2. knock-on effect across school as arts strategies disseminated;
3. TAs more confident generally in dealing with students.

The mix of specialist coaching and mentoring that was displayed worked well for the cohort of teachers involved. It meant that the arts teachers felt that they were doing something that was not only useful, but that the effects of their coaching would quickly be felt in the classroom itself. In the evaluation of the study, a significant number of TAs said that they felt that it was one of the most rewarding and empowering professional development sessions they had attended. Additionally the coaching sessions that followed meant that they felt significantly more a part of the school team and more able to do their job within the classroom in the arts subjects.

Booklet of best practice

A second direct outcome of the professional development and coaching sessions was the generation of a best practice booklet that would be used with new TA staff, detailing the expectations and the types of support that would be given if the individual TA felt a need for it.

***

This chapter has provided teachers with an overview of the content of the book and suggested ways of working with each chapter in order to inquire into best practice for mentoring and coaching to promote professional learning. As teachers develop their own approaches to engaging with the book, they will need to constantly return to the relevant guidelines for working with individual chapters. This will facilitate a dynamic, interactive process allowing teachers to take ownership in directing their own professional learning.

Appendix. Evaluation templates

1.1 Evaluation of collaborative inquiry in mentoring and coaching

Identify the purpose and focus of your inquiry.

What type of professional learning did you explore? (Refer to Chapter 2 to consider whether the learning was academic/knowledge based, learning from experience, learning which links knowledge and experience.)

Identify the key collaborations and processes in your inquiry.

Which mentoring/coaching approaches did you use? (Refer to Chapter 3.)

Identify what you've learned and how you've learned it.

Identify the learning of other key people in the inquiry – what and how.

Evaluate the effectiveness of the mentoring and/or coaching collaboration for the learning.

Are you able to make applications and connections between this experience of professional learning and other areas of your professional life?

Can you identify any future areas for inquiry?

List the evidence you used for this inquiry (policies, useful references/ websites, records etc.).

1.2 The practitioner inquiry spectrum

Collaboration	One-to-one collaboration	⟩⟩⟩⟩⟩⟩⟩⟩⟩⟩	A collaboration involving a group or team
Inquiry	Small-scale inquiry into practice	⟩⟩⟩⟩⟩⟩⟩⟩⟩⟩	Large-scale inquiry into practice
Context	Local context for practice within the institution	⟩⟩⟩⟩⟩⟩⟩⟩⟩⟩	A wider professional context
Criticality	Small-scale question	⟩⟩⟩⟩⟩⟩⟩⟩⟩⟩	A broader question with potential for wider application
Evidence	Small-scale processes for evidence collection	⟩⟩⟩⟩⟩⟩⟩⟩⟩⟩	Multi-faceted processes for collecting evidence
Interpretation	Simple level of interpretation and analysis of evidence	⟩⟩⟩⟩⟩⟩⟩⟩⟩⟩	Complex analysis and interpretation of a well-developed and wide-ranging evidence base
Change/ transformation	Individual change/ transformation	⟩⟩⟩⟩⟩⟩⟩⟩⟩⟩	Broader impact
Dissemination	Limited dissemination within the institution	⟩⟩⟩⟩⟩⟩⟩⟩⟩⟩	High degree of public dissemination

PART I
Theoretical perspectives

2

Dimensions of professional learning

Key learning points

- the purposes of professional learning;
- the nature of professional learning;
- achieving professional learning;
- professional learning, inquiry and mentoring and coaching.

The main aim of mentoring and coaching relationships is to develop professional learning. Therefore any exploration of mentoring and coaching needs to take account of the nature of professional learning. Thus this chapter is concerned with the professional learning of teachers. Our examination of professional learning involves a consideration of the purposes and outcomes (the why), as well as the nature (the what and the how). The chapter concludes by offering a view of mentoring and coaching relationships as a learning platform, a space in which professional learning takes place.

Why professional learning?

In recent years there has been considerable government investment in the professional development of teachers and the wider school workforce at all levels, for example funding for postgraduate professional development, initial teacher education, Masters in Teaching and Learning and leadership pathways programmes provided by the National College for Leadership of Schools and Children's Services (NCLSCS). The majority of professional development associated with these national school workforce policies uses some form of mentoring and coaching as a strategy for developing participants' professional learning. One of the key aims is the improvement of professional practice in relation to national standards of competence in order to enhance the learning and well-being of children and young people's lives. For example the NCLSCS 'works to develop and inspire great leaders of schools, early years settings and children's services so that they can make a positive difference to children's lives' (NCLSCS 2010).

Brockbank and McGill (2006) also recognise the importance of improving professional practice as a result of professional learning. However, they go further in describing three levels of outcome for professional learning. These are improvement, transformation and learning about learning. Learning for improvement uses reflection to improve professional performance and encompasses similar intentions to many of the national programmes. Learning about learning can be compared to Watkins *et al.*'s (1998, 2002) notion of meta-learning which enables learners to stand back and identify how professional learning has been achieved in order to transfer successful learning processes to future situations. Transformation learning is a more radical concept which employs levels of criticality in order to question and challenge existing practices and create new understandings of professional practice and learning. Transformation learning goes further than the improvement of professional performance and allows for the possibility of a critique of underlying ideologies and values which may lead to questioning of national standards and policies as well as of both institutional and individual practices.

What constitutes professional learning?

Professional learning encompasses different types of knowledge and skill. Most providers of professional learning programmes emphasise the importance of experiential learning within the workplace (Marsick and Watkins 1990). This builds on Dewey's (1938) original idea of learning involving experience as well as the acquisition of abstract knowledge. Experiential learning relies on the use of reflection on experience to create new knowledge.

Distinctions between abstract or academic knowledge and experiential knowledge feature in a number of studies of professional learning. Laurillard (1993) outlines three visions of learning as academic, situated and mediated. Academic learning is defined as 'imparted knowledge' which is 'transferred, independent of contexts' and is not necessarily concerned with the application of theory to practice (Ponte 2010: 72). Situated learning includes practical, procedural knowledge acquired in a specific context and understood in relation to that context. Ponte points out the limitations of situated learning as 'learning from experience of what is immediately to hand. Such learning from experience only produces direct, context-based practical knowledge, for direct application; knowledge geared to competent practice and not to describing and understanding reality from a distance'. As a result Ponte (2010) advocates 'mediated learning' from 'articulated knowledge' as the ideal (p. 72).

Mediated learning involves the use of academic knowledge together with reflection on experience in order to transcend the immediate context. Ponte claims that learners 'have to be able to decontextualise such experiences and conceptualise them' (ibid.: 73). Mediated learning involves drawing together knowledge derived from multiple contexts, for example theoretical reading, understanding of policy and reflection on professional practical experience in order to create new knowledge that can then be applied to a broader range of contexts. Ponte (2010) also refers to the work of Popper (1972) to bring a further perspective on the nature of professional learning. Popper uses the metaphor of three worlds as follows: world 3 is a world of 'concepts, theories and abstractions', world 2 is the 'personal, internal world of experience' and world 1 is the world of 'concrete actions in reality', 'the actions that form part of a specific profession'. The professional learner needs to bring together experiences in world 2 and academic knowledge from world 3 in order to improve professional practice within world 1 (ibid.: 74).

These ideas about professional learning depend on a process of constructing new knowledge. The professional learning which takes place within a mentoring or coaching relationship is constructed as a result of social interaction. It is useful to consider social constructivist general learning theory with its emphasis on processes of interaction, collaboration and dialogue as underpinning most effective learning activity. The work of Vygotsky (1978) and Bruner

(1986) highlight the centrality of these processes as Livingston and Schiach (2010) state:

> social interaction helps us to make sense of the world: learning is viewed as a process that involves transmission and reproduction as well as creativity, reflection and transformation ... through social interaction the relationship of people to the world changes as it extends their capacity to interpret and transform it ... social interaction transforms individuals through involvement in collective activities that are culturally and historically situated ... this collaborative approach will result in better outcomes ... by bringing together a range of different perspectives and by explicitly sharing knowledge, those involved have the opportunity to develop mutual understanding ... to create new knowledge and meaning.
>
> (pp. 85–6)

Thus professional learning through the social interaction of mentoring and coaching affords greater opportunities to bring together knowledge and experience from the multiple contexts of mediated learning.

This chapter is mostly concerned with professional learning which encompasses knowledge and skill and the role of experience; however, it is also important to acknowledge the ways in which individual affective aspects such as confidence, self-esteem and trust contribute to the nature of the professional learning. The work of Gardener (1983) on multiple intelligence and Goleman (1995) on emotional intelligence highlight the importance of understanding and managing the emotions in professional contexts. Goleman identified five 'domains' of emotional intelligence which can be summarized as recognizing and understanding one's own and other emotions as well as managing emotions and motivating oneself. Some of the emotional factors are discussed by Brockbank and McGill (2006) when they consider the affective aspects of mentoring and coaching particularly in relation to the skills required.

How is professional learning achieved?

Carnell *et al.* (2006), in a study of mentoring and coaching in higher education linked to a programme designed to support teachers' development of academic writing skills, cite three models of learning developed from Watkins *et al.* (2002). These three models are:

1. instruction model (learning by teaching);
2. construction model (learning by understanding);
3. co-construction model (learning through dialogue).

Whilst the instruction and construction models are ones which may contribute to successful professional learning, it is the co-construction model which is closest to the experiential, mediated learning engaged with through the social process of mentoring and coaching.

Watkins also draws on the seminal model of experiential learning developed by David Kolb (1984). This model proposes a four-stage learning cycle which moves from actual experience to reflection on this experience, to a process of learning and reconceptualisation, ending with a stage of acting on the outcomes of this process. The Kolb cycle enables understanding of what happens when adults are engaged in learning and change.

This model can be used to clarify the processes of experiential learning. Kolb's model is particularly relevant to experiential learning because it links experience with developing professional expertise through a cycle of experience, reflection, conceptualisation and application. This cycle is continuously repeated as new knowledge arises from reflection on concrete experiences based on action. Kolb's model is not concerned with mediated learning as the emphasis lies solely on knowledge gained through experience rather than including academic knowledge. Watkins recognizes Kolb's work on learning as 'the process of creating knowledge by making sense of experience' (Watkins *et al.* 1998: 21); however, he adds to this four-stage learning cycle a cycle of meta-learning which he defines as 'the process of making sense of your experience of learning' (ibid.). This concern for learning about learning is a useful addition to Kolb's cycle when considering the processes for developing professional learning which has the potential to be transferred to other contexts.

What characterises successful professional learning for teachers?

Successful professional learning needs to take account of pedagogical approaches to adult learning. The work of Knowles (1980) identified the importance of a high-level of autonomy for successful adult learning including the self-evaluation of learning. This is recognised in the work of Carnell and Lodge (2002) on the identification of effective teacher learning. They state that effective teacher learning experiences arise when teachers have ownership of the learning process and work to develop shared aims and outcomes. Carnell and Lodge also emphasise the importance of the day to day work context, as well as of opportunities for reflection, learning and change. They recognise the need for teacher dialogue and collaboration to develop actions for change.

We have identified three key components of successful professional learning for teachers. These are reflection, dialogue and criticality.

Reflection

An essential component of the work of both Kolb and Watkins is reflection on practice and learning. Reflective learning as a basis for professional learning has been central to the work of many professional fields including education. The work of Schön (1983) has formed the basis for many approaches to reflective practice. He states:

> The practitioner allows himself to experience surprise, puzzlement, or confusion in a situation which he finds uncertain or unique. He reflects on the phenomenon before him, and on the prior understandings which have been implicit in his behaviour. He carries out an experiment which serves to generate both a new understanding of the phenomenon and a change in the situation.
>
> (p. 68)

Dietz (1998) draws on Schön's work in developing four levels for a professional learning cycle which uses reflection as a final level in a process of inquiry about practice. This cycle begins with consideration of the 'learning territory' or context, moves into the 'organisation' level of collecting evidence and applying, then to adapting practice as a result of findings. Boud (1993) also developed a cyclic model using reflection on experience and pre-experience as the final stage in the learning process.

Recently there has been a growing critical voice about the ways in which reflection has been hijacked by professions and in the process lost its original critical intentions. Reflection has become a tool for professional control: 'the original idea of reflection as a tool for critical praxis is reversed and instead it becomes a tool for control and orthodoxy' (Kilminster *et al.* 2010: 3).

One way of challenging the uncritical use of reflection is to use the process of reflection to question underlying assumptions and values. Argyris and Schön (1996) used the term 'double-loop learning' to go beyond improvement in professional practice via reflection 'to bring about a profound shift in underlying values by cracking their paradigms or "ways of seeing the world"' (Brockbank and McGill 2006: 33). A further challenge is found in the work of Boud (2010) who says that notions of reflection have traditionally been based in 'an overly individualistic view of learning' and argues for 'alternative conceptions that view reflection within the context of settings which necessarily have more of a group- or team- based work orientation' (p. 25). He identifies major features of the changing context of professional practice to be its collaborative rather than individual nature and 'an increasing emphasis on practice being co-produced' (p. 30). This view of professional learning as being co-constructed reflection is highly relevant to a process of critical inquiry through mentoring and coaching.

Dialogue

A key process in the co-construction of professional learning is the use of dialogue. Dialogue can be seen as an internal dialogue where an individual engages in personal reflection to achieve an insight (Clutterbuck 1998); however, the most relevant dialogic process within a mentoring and coaching relationship takes place in collaboration. As Brockbank and McGill state, it adds 'external dialogue to the inner dialogue by providing another perspective, asking questions not previously considered and drawing on other experience' (ibid.: 54). Transformative learning according to Brockbank and McGill is more likely to occur as a result of collaborative dialogue.

Bohm (1996) has explored the nature of dialogue and contrasts dialogue with discussion, seeing dialogue as a process where meaning is socially constructed through collaboration and is constantly changing. In discussion individual ideas are asserted but a collaborative outcome is not necessarily intended.

Brockbank and McGill link Belenky *et al.*'s (1986) notions of 'separated' and 'connected knowing' with Bohm's distinction between discussion and dialogue. The idea of connected knowing links to Bohm's view of dialogue as a creation of meaning through collaborative interaction. As Clinchy stated in 1996, dialogic discourse takes place between 'allies, even advocates, of the position they are examining' (p. 208) and understanding the perspective of the other in the dialogue is an important step in this creation of meaning.

However, for Brockbank and McGill (2006) the aim of dialogue in professional learning is to effect a transformation in the learning through the collaboration. This is an important outcome of Brockbank and McGill's 'evolutionary mentoring' which is discussed in Chapter 3. Dialogue is an essential vehicle for the reflective learning described by Brockbank and McGill at all three levels (for improvement, for transformation and for learning about learning). Dialogue with another is more able to bring about transformative learning through engaging at the edge of assumptions and beliefs and the possibility of constructivist learning as well as learning about learning (p. 56). In his discussion about reflection which is co-constructed in transdisciplinary relationships (such as those often found in mentoring and coaching), Boud (2010) describes the challenge of 'creating common ground' (p. 34). This process 'involves the questioning of the taken-for-granted assumptions arising from the particular disciplinary background of the members . . . being able to step aside from one situation and view it from the perspective of another' (ibid.). In our view this produces the inquiring state of mind which is an essential component of criticality.

Criticality

Our third key process, criticality, is highly dependent on the development of an inquiring state of mind. Slavit and Nelson (2009) discuss Jaworski's (2006) 'notions of inquiry as a tool and inquiry as a way of being' in order to clarify the meaning of an inquiring state of mind or 'inquiry stance' (p. 7). They identify a 'disposition to ponder and seek transformation' as underpinning the notion of an 'inquiry stance' (p. 8). Thus the development of teacher criticality as a way of being requires a long-term process of reflection 'given that an inquiry stance is naturally related to both teaching and beliefs about teaching' (Jaworski 2006, in Slavit and Nelson 2009: 8). The development of criticality within professional learning is greatly enhanced by collaboration and interaction. Wells (1999) highlights the crucial importance of collaboration and Slavit and Nelson (2009) use this to demonstrate the collaborative contribution to criticality: 'a willingness to wonder, to ask questions, and to seek to understand by collaborating with others in the attempt to make answers to them' (Wells 1999: 121). Nelson (2005) goes further by identifying how taking an inquiry stance can lead to the co-construction of meaning. His use of the term 'knowledge negotiation' (Slavit and Nelson 2009: 8) as a process of examining 'alternative perspectives and questioning one's own knowledge and beliefs' (ibid.) complements Jaworski's ideas of the inquiry stance being related to teachers' beliefs. As well as consideration of individual knowledge and beliefs, Fook (2010) includes consideration of 'dominant or hegemonic assumptions' which may unwittingly influence professional practice and learning. In her discussion of the theory of critical reflection she also sees criticality as strongly related to transformative learning and cites Cranton (1996) 'to involve and lead to some fundamental change in perspective' (pp. 79-80). Other earlier considerations of transformative learning also highlight the ways in which critical reflection as a social process can lead to the development of new knowledge and interpretations with the potential to impact on future action. Mezirow (1994) discusses 'a new or revised interpretation of the meaning of one's experience as a guide to action' (pp. 222–3) and similarly Cranton (1996) sees transformative learning as a process of critical reflection which leads to action.

Where does the professional learning take place?

In order to bring together the three key processes of reflection, dialogue and criticality within the professional learning that takes place in mentoring and coaching relationships, it is helpful to conceptualise a metaphorical space where these processes can take place. Hulme and Cracknell (2010) use 'third space' and 'hybridity' theories in order to conceptualise a space for the exploration of 'professional cultural exchange and the development of trans-professional knowledge' (p. 56). They describe 'hybridity' as examining 'the condition of being 'in-between' several different sources of knowledge'(p. 57), stating that 'Hybridity applies to the integration of competing knowledge and discourses; to the reading and writing of texts and to individual and social spaces, contexts and relationships' (ibid.). They conclude that it is important to have a 'space for dialogue between participants that is safe, secure and supportive, space that "stands outside" the formal areas of practice'. They use Bhabha's (1994) ideas of the space being 'an innovative site of collaboration, and contestation where border discourse takes place' (p. 56).

Smith (2000) applies the metaphor of a platform to a notion of space for dialogue leading to professional learning within initial teacher education programmes. Ponte (2010) describes Smith's (2000) notion of the platform as

> goals, content, methods and organisational measures which create a meeting place, where ... others can learn from each other and engage in debate. The central idea is that the participants consult each other to decide what they will learn and how.
>
> (Ponte 2010: 71)

Ponte (2007) applies the metaphor of the platform to postgraduate programmes for continuing teacher education. She identifies critical inquiry as an essential process and goal for professional learning with a number of interactions between different types of knowledge and its application taking place on the platform (p. 74).

Smith's (2000) and Ponte's (2007) notions of the platform can also be applied to the professional learning which takes place in mentoring and coaching where each encounter could be viewed as a 'programme' for professional learning where participants meet to determine goals and processes for critical inquiry leading to reciprocal professional learning. Given the diversity of knowledge and experience that is brought to the process of professional learning, the learning that takes place on the platform is not necessarily unproblematic. Ponte (2010: 72) describes how this learning is constantly in tension. For example, as noted in Chapter 3, there may be a tension for teachers between intrinsically (self-) motivated learning and extrinsically directed, externally regulated learning. However, the platform is a place where tensions such as these can be explored through collaboration and dialogue.

The metaphor of a learning platform for developing a critical inquiry approach to professional learning through mentoring and coaching relationships allows for the creation of new (mediated) knowledge through the social process of co-construction using reflection, dialogue and criticality. This chapter began by examining the different types of knowledge which constitute professional learning (e.g. Popper's three worlds and Laurillard's three visions). The platform provides a space for the interaction between these different types of knowledge in the pursuit of transformative professional learning. The mentoring and coaching relationship can be seen as the learning platform which enables collaborative critical inquiry to take place.

3

Mentoring and coaching: a platform for professional learning

Key learning points

- the terms mentoring and coaching;
- the nature and purposes of mentoring and coaching;
- the development and use of mentoring and coaching for professional learning in schools;
- a new way forward to develop professional learning within mentoring and coaching.

This chapter poses fundamental questions about the purposes and philosophies associated with mentoring and coaching being used to develop professional learning in schools. It then examines current practices arising from national policies which determine much of the practice in mentoring and coaching in schools at the moment. Finally the chapter explores the metaphor of a learning platform as a space for interaction between different types of knowledge in the pursuit of transformative professional learning. This builds on discussions from the previous chapter which link the platform metaphor to a process for professional learning within mentoring and coaching relationships.

Mentoring and coaching – are they separate concepts?

Garvey *et al.* (2009) highlight 'the confusing array of definitions found in modern discourses' (p. 27) relating to mentoring and coaching and identify a huge overlap between mentoring and coaching. Brockbank and McGill (2006) also state that the 'terminology of mentoring and coaching in the literature has been confused and confusing' (p. 1). Attempts to make distinctions between mentoring and coaching have failed to produce agreed understandings of the definitions of these terms and in many models the terms would appear to be interchangeable. Brockbank and McGill (2006) suggest that mentoring and coaching practices can be examined by asking questions about the purpose, process and learning outcome. However their classification of mentoring and coaching into functionalist, engagement, revolutionary or evolutionary approaches is not used to distinguish between the terms mentoring and coaching. They argue that the choice of the specific term 'is irrelevant' (p. 275) as their concern is for mentoring and coaching activity to clearly identify purpose, process and learning outcome. Garvey *et al.* (2009) support the integration of the terms advocated by the European Mentoring and Coaching Council and have coined the term 'one-to-one developmental dialogue' (p. 224) to describe all mentoring and coaching relationships. They also suggest that 'the meaning of coaching and mentoring is fundamentally determined by the social context' (p. 25) and use a range of dimensions first suggested by Garvey in 1994 which focus on the nature and quality of the relationship, its organisation and purpose to analyse how the relationships within mentoring and coaching are dynamic and change over time.

This book has not advocated a clear distinction between the terms mentoring and coaching and frequently cites them together. However, in Part II the inquiries tend to use coaching for more specifically focused short-term collaborations and mentoring for broader longer-term relationships.

What are the purposes of mentoring and coaching?

Any attempt at consideration of the purposes of mentoring and coaching is challenged by what Colley (2003: 13) describes as 'a practice that remains ill-defined, poorly conceptualised, and weakly theorised, leading to confusion in policy and practice'. The purposes of mentoring and coaching in different professional areas are inevitably underpinned by professional cultures and philosophies which are not always explicit but will impact on approaches used in mentoring and coaching relationships. Brockbank and McGill (2006) state: 'the method of mentoring or coaching is likely to be influenced by the philosophy that underpins it, and in general the theoretical base is implicit and undeclared' (p. 9). However, common purposes of mentoring and coaching in any professional context usually include two key areas:

1. developing a process of professional learning;
2. achieving a level of individual or institutional change.

In an educational context there are two prevailing philosophies which underpin mentoring and coaching approaches. The first is a behaviourist stance which presents fixed definitions and purposes in order to produce improvement in professional performance either at an individual or institutional level. This is similar to Brockbank and McGill's classification of functionalist approaches to mentoring and coaching where the key purpose is to improve individual or institutional performance to serve the 'perceived "needs" of the organisation or society' (p. 12) with minimal questioning of established values and norms. Brockbank and McGill also identify engagement mentoring or coaching as a 'humanistic version of functionalist mentoring or coaching' (p. 13).

The second prevailing philosophy is informed by much educational research where the social constructivist approach originally conceived by Vygotsky (1978) underpins the dominant discourse around professional learning. Here a key purpose of mentoring and coaching is the social construction of new professional knowledge in order to inform individual and institutional change. This approach can be related to Brockbank and McGill's evolutionary approach to mentoring and coaching in which underlying values and power structures can be challenged in order to bring about transformation at individual or institutional levels. Brockbank and McGill identify this evolutionary approach as one which is 'usually (but not always) found in private arrangements, often quite separate from the workplace, where professional mentors or coaches work over time, to an agreed contract' (p. 14). In Chapter 4, as an extension to this, we argue that an approach to professional learning which uses critical collaborative inquiry within a mentoring and coaching relationship has the potential to effect the transformation identified by Brockbank and McGill, within an education institution.

What does mentoring and coaching involve?

Differences in purpose or underlying philosophy will also be accompanied by differences of overall approach to mentoring and coaching. Clutterbuck (2003), in an attempt to provide a more consistent framework for examining mentoring and coaching policy and practices, identifies three key variables as context, process and outcome.

Context

Clutterbuck (2003) recognises that contextual factors will impact on the mentoring and coaching purposes. In applying this to mentoring and coaching for education, a consideration of context will include the following:

- location factors might relate to issues such as socio-economic variables, diversity issues, urban or rural environments, the availability of physical space for the mentoring and coaching relationship to take place;
- the extent to which internal or external personnel contribute;
- status, diversity and power factors such as gender, ethnicity, disability and organisational features such as contracts, policies and degree of formality;
- individual, institutional and societal goals;
- quality of relationships;
- underlying values and power relations;
- dominant discourses used within the institution.

Process

Clutterbuck (2003) recognises that variables of process can have a major impact on the outcomes of a mentoring and coaching relationship. We identify the following process variables as significant factors that impact on the outcomes:

- strategies used in organising mentoring relationships such as frequency of meetings, uses of technology, record keeping;
- the nature and quality of the dialogue;
- the nature and quality of the collaboration;

- the use of different approaches such as the inquiry-based approach through investigation, reflection and questioning, which is proposed in Chapter 4 of this book;
- the underlying model of professional learning.

Outcome

Clutterbuck (2003) discusses the importance of a relationship between outcomes and goals in a mentoring and coaching relationship and recognises that different types of relationship will have different expectations of outcomes. Consideration of outcome includes:

- the nature of the learning resulting from the mentoring and coaching process (this might be learning of specific professional knowledge or meta-learning arising from the process, for example learning related to the development of dialogue and collaboration);
- the development of the professional learning relationship as a collaborative process;
- the degree and nature of the resulting impact or change at individual and/or institutional levels;
- the potential for generalisation and/or transfer to other contexts;
- any unexpected outcomes, gains or disappointments.

Clutterbuck's (2003) framework of context, process and outcome has been used as an organisational structure for the inquiries reported in Chapters 6 to 8 of this book.

How have schools developed mentoring and coaching for professional learning?

Mentoring and coaching has been part of educational practice for a number of years. Texts on mentoring and coaching frequently cite examples from mythology and historical sources to locate mentoring and coaching within a historical tradition (see, e.g. Garvey *et al.* 2009: 9–27). However, this book is concerned with recent developments in the use of mentoring and coaching in schools. In the last few years there has been a considerable growth and investment in processes of mentoring and coaching at all levels, including policy, practice and theoretical research. In the last two decades national policy changes to the training and development of teachers have led to an increasing formalisation of mentoring and coaching processes and relationships. These processes have affected trainees and teachers from initial teacher training through to senior leadership development.

It was in the early 1990s that the formal requirements for partnership working within initial teacher training established the use of experienced teachers as mentors providing school-based training and support. These requirements were a result of both research and policy developments. In their book *Subject Mentoring in the Secondary School*, Arthur *et al.* (1997) show how processes for the mentoring of trainee teachers arose from the development of different partnership structures between schools and higher-education institutions. They cite the 'internship scheme' developed at Oxford University in 1987 as a model of collaborative partnership which led to a reflective practitioner model of discursive mentoring within teacher education. They compare this with a competence-based model which tended to produce what Arthur *et al.* refer to as 'pragmatic mentoring' (p. 95).

Since this time, mentoring and coaching has come to be seen as a key professional development tool from the first year of teaching through to preparation for headship. It is also now widely used as part of the widening of the school workforce agenda both in professional development and as a strategy for working with school students in order to develop motivation and aspiration. Mentoring and coaching is also used in a wide range of school contexts for a variety of purposes. These include:

- Initial teacher training, which uses formal mentoring relationships as a key part of the training process.
- In the early and continuing professional development of teachers, mentoring and coaching has gained predominance. Newly qualified teachers (NQTs) are assigned a school-based mentor and the Masters in Teaching and Learning programme first introduced as a pilot in 2009 and rolled out nationally in 2010 requires M-level coaches to be trained and identified within school settings.
- Leadership programmes offered by the National College for Leadership of Schools and Children's Services, such as the

'National Professional Qualification for Headship', 'Leading from the Middle', and 'Leadership Pathways', all use coaching as an essential tool for professional development.

- Executive coaching at senior leadership level is used for the specific development of the individual but also for broader institutional aims.
- Learning mentors are a well-established part of the wider school workforce and are often used to support school students with learning or behavioural difficulties in order to reduce disaffection and improve attitudes.
- Coaching is also used in schools to develop specific abilities, skills and talents in specialised areas such as sports and music.

What framework underpins mentoring and coaching in schools?

In 2005 a 'National Framework for Mentoring and Coaching' was developed, drawing on the work of the Centre for the Use of Research Evidence in Education (CUREE). This has been endorsed by a number of influential organisations, including the Department for Education (formerly the Department for Children, Schools and Families (DCSF)), the General Teaching Council (GTC), the National College for Leadership of Schools and Children's Services (NCLSCS), the Primary and Secondary National Strategies and the Training and Development Agency (TDA). The Framework arose from a study by CUREE in 2004–5 giving an overview of research into professional development and the contribution of mentoring and coaching to successful professional learning.

The framework includes ten principles of mentoring and coaching, core concepts for mentoring and coaching and skills for mentoring and coaching. There is also a comparison of the overlapping roles involved in mentoring and coaching. The framework has been designed to help increase the impact of continuing professional development on student learning, arising as it does from a number of studies on professional development, notably Joyce and Showers (2002), Cordingley *et al.* (2003) and Adey *et al.* (2004).

How useful is this framework?

The ten principles identified in the framework are as follows:

- a learning conversation;
- a thoughtful relationship;
- a learning agreement;
- combining support from fellow professional learners and specialists;
- growing self-direction;
- setting challenging and personal goals;
- understanding why different approaches work;
- acknowledging the benefits to the mentors and coaches;
- experimenting and observing;
- using resources effectively.

This is a useful list for describing mentoring and coaching relationships and activity; however, it is not a list of underlying principles. Rather it is a mixture of functions, processes and outcomes.

The framework also identifies three core concepts, namely mentoring, specialist coaching and co-coaching. However, these are roles rather than concepts. This part of the framework omits key concepts which can inform the mentoring and coaching process, such as collaboration and the nature of professional knowledge and learning. The skills listed in the framework provide useful guidance for mentors, coaches and professional learners but are limited in their potential for collaborative learning. There is also limited scope for criticality and reciprocal learning.

Thus the framework reduces the complexity of the original research findings to a more simplistic categorisation of mentoring and coaching functions and roles.

How is mentoring and coaching used in schools?

It is useful at this point to examine in more detail four key areas where mentoring and coaching take place within a school context. These are:

- initial teacher education;
- early and continuing professional development;

- leadership;
- wider school workforce.

Initial teacher education

Within initial teacher education there is a statutory requirement for a substantial part of the training to take place in schools to enable trainee teachers to demonstrate that they have met the standards for Qualified Teacher Status (TDA 2008: R2.8). There is also a requirement for providers of initial teacher training to work in partnership in order 'to ensure that partners work together to contribute to the selection, training and assessment of trainee teachers against the QTS standards' (R3.2). Currently the way in which teacher-training providers interpret this requirement for partnership with schools is through the use of an experienced teacher being identified to work alongside a trainee teacher as a mentor during school-based work experience. Traditionally these experienced teachers or mentors are given training for their role by the training provider, often a higher-education institution.

This interpretation of partnership working has its roots in a statement from the Secretary of State for Education and Science in England who in January 1992 announced that 'schools should play a much larger part in initial teacher training as full partners of higher education institutions' (DfE 1992).

Responses to this call for increased school involvement in initial teacher training drew on the model of the Oxford internship scheme (cited earlier) and led to a plethora of writing, for example, Hagger et al. (1993), Watkins and Whalley (1993), Furlong and Maynard (1995) and Arthur et al. (1997), all interpreting the school-based role as focused around the work of an experienced teacher appointed as a mentor to the trainee.

This mentoring role has continued to be recognised as key to the processes involved in school-based teacher training and in maintaining partnerships between schools and training providers. However, it tends to be the responsibility of higher-education institution training providers to decide how to work with schools to define the role. Increasingly a number of government-initiated projects have been set up to develop the training role of schools such as training schools, partnership development schools and the 'Beyond Partnership' project set up by the TDA as a consultation in 2009. These projects have all sought to develop further the role of the school-based mentor. However, there has so far been no significant national review or guidance on the effective use of a mentor in initial teacher training and the terms used for professional learning roles tend to vary. Official documents (e.g. TDA 2009a) tend to use terms such as 'school partners' or 'school-based tutors' in order to construct the teacher as an equal partner in teacher training provided by universities. However, the case studies used to illustrate this guidance demonstrate the extent to which the term 'mentor' has become accepted without question as the common currency. There is therefore scope for debating issues around the role of a mentor within initial teacher training and the nature and quality of the mentoring collaboration.

Early and continuing professional development

The recent picture for the early and continuing professional development of teachers has become very different from that of initial teacher education as a result of the development of two initiatives. The first of these is the DCSF (2008) guidance on NQT induction which requires a school-based induction tutor to 'provide, or co-ordinate, guidance and effective support including coaching and mentoring for the NQT's professional development'. The second is the development of a coaching strategy for the effective delivery of the new government-initiated 'Masters in Teaching and Learning' (MTL) (TDA 2009b). This strategy has been developed 'to demonstrate the TDA's vision for the role of the MTL school-based coach'.

The 'Masters in Teaching and Learning' document provides a much more explicit model of partnership between schools and higher education as 'MTL providers' and identifies a clearer role for the school-based coach as an MTL tutor. Like the induction tutor, the school-based coach will be expected to provide 'support and professional challenge' but the role has been further defined to include a need to 'motivate and inspire, encourage on-going enquiry and reflection ... identifying needs relevant to the participants' school contexts, apply evidence and educational theory to real-life situations' (ibid.: 4).

Within both induction and MTL, the mentoring and coaching role is seen as separate from the other professional relationships which might exist between the mentor/coach and the early career teachers. The training for coaching within MTL is firmly based on the 'National Framework for mentoring and coaching' (DCSF 2005). Our critique of the limitations of this model (see pp. 35–6) suggests that it is unlikely to fulfil the more challenging aspirations of the coaching strategy for collaborative inquiry, reflection and professional learning. With the introduction of the MTL, national frameworks for early and continuing professional development for teachers show a clear shift from use of the term mentoring to that of coaching.

Leadership

Coaching has also become a key tool for professional development in national school leadership programmes such as those offered by the NCLSCS. These include the 'National Professional Qualification for Headship', 'Leading from the Middle', and 'Leadership Pathways'. These programmes identify some common aims for coaching individual participants such as:

- facilitating participants' in-school learning;
- challenging participants to extend their practice and develop their skills in a number of ways;
- establishing a trusting and purposeful relationship with participants;
- the use of on-line communities and materials.

All these programmes have clear guidelines for the role of the coach and expect the coach to be an experienced professional who has received specific training for the role.

Executive coaching programmes are also sometimes used by schools at senior leadership level for the specific development of the individual in order to enable institutional development. These programmes tend to operate outside of the usual government accountability structures with a focus on individual support and challenge. An example of such a coaching programme is given in Chapter 7.

Coaching at this level often makes use of models used by a range of professions such as the GROW model (Whitmore 1996) or the Skilled Helper model (Egan 1990) to structure a process of goal-setting and consideration of options to support individual professional learning.

Wider school workforce

In the TDA (2009c) publication 'Strategy for the Professional Development of the Children's Workforce in schools 2009–12' the National Advisory Group for the professional development of the children's workforce identifies coaching and mentoring as a feature of professional development for the wider school workforce (p. 11). In this document coaching and mentoring is also linked to improving outcomes for children and young people and the performance review cycle for the school workforce is underpinned by a culture of 'coaching for performance'. The case studies in this document include the identification of a 'Performance Coach' and coaching to support a collaborative culture in school. The document also calls for research to show the impact on children and young people of professional development which includes mentoring and coaching .

What is the argument for a different set of principles to underpin mentoring and coaching in schools?

If we return to our earlier discussion of the purposes of professional learning in Chapter 2, the discourse in the national frameworks for mentoring and coaching in schools tends to present more fixed purposes and behaviourist definitions of mentoring and coaching with an emphasis on improvement of individual or institutional practice. There tends to be less emphasis on criticality and the collaborative co-construction of new professional knowledge in these national models.

In Chapter 2 we considered the metaphor of a platform used by Smith (2000) and Ponte (2007) as useful for conceptualising an 'alternative' space where mentoring and coaching relationships can take place. In order to facilitate professional learning which is critically and collaboratively co-constructed through mentoring and coaching we have identified the following principles to inform the way participants in a mentoring and coaching relationship could operate on the platform. These are:

- attempts to develop coherence between theoretical knowledge and personal and professional knowledge and experience;
- the ability of participants with varying levels and types of knowledge and professional experience to engage in dialogue and collaborative reflection;
- the co-construction of new professional knowledge;
- an understanding that the platform is a place of shared goals and principles that are continuously reviewed and contested.

However, these four principles are not enough, and in Chapter 4 we consider how professional learning which occurs within mentoring and coaching relationships can be enhanced through the process of critical inquiry. This chapter will show how two additional principles; first, the achievement of professional learning through processes of critical inquiry, and second, critical inquiry as both process and goal are intrinsic to the notion of the platform. By emphasising criticality, these two additional principles enhance the collaborative co-construction of professional knowledge in a mentoring and coaching relationship.

4

Practitioner inquiry for professional learning in mentoring and coaching

Key learning points

- the nature of action research and practitioner research;
- the choice of the term practitioner inquiry;
- practitioner inquiry and professional learning;
- a spectrum for different levels of practitioner inquiry;
- professional inquiry and mentoring and coaching.

The aim of this book is to examine how the professional learning which occurs within mentoring and coaching relationships can be enhanced. In Chapter 2 we have already highlighted the importance of dialogue, reflection and criticality for professional learning. One way of linking these three aspects of professional learning is through a process of critical inquiry. Thus this chapter will examine the critical inquiry process which could operate at a number of levels from critical questioning to carrying out more sustained practitioner research.

Campbell and McNamara (2010) offer a model of professional learning which constructs critical inquiry as practitioner inquiry and embraces practitioner research and some elements of action research. For the purposes of this book therefore we have adopted the term practitioner inquiry as a generic term but draw on the literature related to action research and practitioner research in our discussion of the theoretical frameworks underlying these methodologies. In order to define what we mean by practitioner inquiry we need to examine some definitions of action research and its links to practitioner research.

What are action research and practitioner research?

The terms action research and practitioner research are frequently used interchangeably and the principles, purposes and processes are difficult to distinguish within the literature. In their discussion of practitioner research Campbell and McNamara (2010) refer to 'the plethora of terms used to describe practitioner research and inquiry and related professional learning in educational contexts' (p. 10). They suggest that this presents a 'complex and messy picture' (ibid.). Campbell (2007) also states that 'Practitioner research is closely related to, and draws on, the methodologies of the "family of action research"' described by Kemmis and McTaggart (2005: 560).

Practitioner research and action research can be distinguished from other forms of research through the aim of 'improving rather than proving as an approach to research' (Campbell 2007: 1). The tradition of action research in the UK can be traced back to the work of Lawrence Stenhouse (1975) who developed action research as an approach to studying the theory and practice of teaching and the curriculum. There are a number of accounts of the development of this tradition, for example Zeichner (2001) and Hopkins (2002). Since the early days of action research, practitioner research has come to represent an approach to professional learning in education which is increasingly widely used.

Campbell (2007) draws on the work of Stenhouse (1975), Elliott (1991), Cochran-Smith and Lytle (1993), and Zeichner and Noffke (2001) to highlight the following key features of practitioner research:

- a focus on teachers' work and teachers themselves as a basis for research;
- the employment of critical reflection and systematic study of practice;
- control and ownership of the research by the practitioner.

Koshy (2005) uses the term action research to describe the process of research by practitioners (pp. 3–10). She summarises the interpretations of a number of researchers and emphasises the importance of the following features:

- it is an investigation of practice owned by the researcher;
- it is situated in the researcher's professional context;
- it is emergent, cyclical and participatory;
- it is aimed at solving problems, improving practice and facilitating change;
- it constructs theory from practice through analysis, reflection and evaluation;
- it operates at the level of individuals or groups.

These features can be found with different degrees of emphasis in the definitions used by a range of theorists. An emphasis on improvement of practice through reflection on action can be found in the work of Carr and Kemmis (1986) and Ebbutt (1985). For example, Carr and Kemmis (1986) state 'Action research is simply a form of self-reflective enquiry undertaken by participants in social situations in order to improve the rationality and justice of their own practices, and the situations in which the practices are carried out' (p. 162). Cohen and Mannion (1994) demonstrate the situated, emergent nature of action research when they describe it as

> an on-the-spot procedure designed to deal with a concrete problem located in an immediate situation. This means that ideally, the step-by-step process is constantly monitored over varying periods of time and by a variety of mechanisms ... so that the ensuing feedback may be translated into modifications, adjustment, directional changes, redefinitions, as necessary, so as to bring lasting benefit to the ongoing process itself rather than to some future occasion.
>
> (p. 192)

Reason and Bradbury (2001) discuss the importance of evidence collection and analysis to the process. They describe action research as an iterative inquiry process which balances collaborative problem solving actions with data-driven analysis or research in order to understand underlying issues and enable predictions about personal and organisational change. O'Leary (2004) considers the relationship between theory and practice and identifies action research as 'A strategy that pursues action and knowledge in an integrated fashion through a cyclical and participatory process. In action research processes, outcome and application are inextricably linked' (p. 139). Koshy (2005) also reveals how knowledge is constructed and disseminated as a result of the action research process by stating:

> I consider action research as a constructive enquiry, during which the researcher constructs his or her knowledge of specific issues through planning, acting, evaluating, refining and learning from experience. It is a continuous learning process in which the researcher learns and also shares the newly generated knowledge with those who may benefit from it.
>
> (p. 9)

Some researchers such as Elliott (1991), Reason and Bradbury (2001) and Zeichner (2003) highlight the importance of collaboration as part of the practitioner research process. Elliott sees collaboration as essential to action research by teachers in order to avoid a focus merely on technical skills. Collaborative action research has the potential to empower teachers to 'critique the curriculum structures which shape their practices and the power to negotiate change within the system that maintains them' (p. 55). The collaborative nature of practitioner research is not always prioritised; however, this book emphasises the importance of the collaborative process in any investigation within mentoring and coaching as mentoring and coaching inevitably involves collaboration.

Why use the term 'practitioner inquiry'?

Campbell and McNamara (2010) state that practitioner research is a more useful generic term than action research to describe the range of possible approaches that could be adopted by teachers to develop changes and improvements within professional learning and practice. However, from the definitions in the literature it is difficult to make clear distinctions between action research and practitioner research. It is not the intention of this book to address this complexity of terminology and therefore we have adopted Campbell's use of the term 'practitioner inquiry' (ibid.: 15) to allow for the broadest range of types of investigation which might be useful to professional learning in the workplace. The term 'practitioner research' also suggests a longer-term and more complex process than a simple one-off inquiry into an individual's practice within a single context and thus the term 'practitioner inquiry' covers a broader range of scale of teacher inquiry. This range is demonstrated in the model on page 49 and discussed later in this chapter. Practitioner inquiry, like action research and practitioner research focuses on both the theoretical and the practical for teachers' professional learning. Groundwater-Smith and Mockler (2006: 107) emphasise that 'those involved in practitioner inquiry are bound to engage with both "theoretical" and "practical" knowledge moving seamlessly between the two'.

How does practitioner inquiry link to professional learning?

Most models of action and practitioner research are cyclical, showing the research cycle as an iterative process applied to action and practice. Similarly, the professional learning models discussed in Chapter 2 are cyclical and iterative, showing a process of reflection on knowledge and experience linked to action. The action research models produced by Kemmis and McTaggart (2005) and O'Leary (2004), for example, show change occurring via a process of planning for change, acting and observing the process and results of the change, reflecting on the processes and then revising the plan to begin the process again. An earlier model by Elliot (1991) provides a detailed process of step-by-step analysis and amendment of planned actions resulting from this. Both these models imply that professional learning is taking place via the processes of reflection, analysis and revision embedded in the cycle. Thus the process of inquiry within the research cycle links directly to professional learning outcomes.

Practitioner inquiry enables teachers to develop disciplined inquiry into professional practice in order to inform and improve their practice. This inquiry formulates action to address identified issues and then evaluates the effects and impact on practice of this action. Practitioner inquiry requires teachers to adopt an inquiring state of mind in order to study and ask questions about practice in context and thereby understand, improve and transform practice. Practitioner inquiry enables teachers to maintain a degree of professional autonomy and judgment through the requirement to 'problem set as well as problem solve' (Blackmore 2002: 17).

What is the nature of practitioner inquiry?

In this book practitioner inquiry is interpreted as a collaborative process which covers eight key elements. These are:

1. *Collaboration.* Teachers work together to develop reciprocal professional learning.
2. *Inquiry.* Teachers investigate an aspect of professional practice.
3. *Context.* Teachers are aware of their context and role and participate as agents of change within the context of their practice.
4. *Criticality.* Teachers raise questions about practice.
5. *Evidence.* Teachers systematically collect evidence, in order to support the process of inquiry.
6. *Interpretation.* Teachers analyse and interpret the evidence collected.
7. *Potential for change/transformation.* Teachers identify and reflect on the resulting change or transformations in practice.
8. *Dissemination.* Teachers share their findings.

These eight elements can be represented as a spectrum. Table 4.1 shows these eight elements and the continuum between the smallest level inquiry and a more substantial extended practitioner inquiry. At its crudest level a small-scale inquiry would include all the features on the left of the spectrum and an extended inquiry would include all the features to the right of the spectrum. However, in reality the spectrum allows for more fluidity on a continuum between the two extremes and for variability on the continuum between the eight elements. So, for example, a small-scale question might contain significant potential for wider application with a limited evidence base. A teacher may want to find out if there is potential for peer coaching between newly qualified teachers (NQTs) in the science department to improve their time management in relation to lesson preparation. The context for the inquiry is small scale because it is focusing on two NQTs in one department, and this will provide a limited evidence base. However, the inquiry may produce findings relevant to other NQTs in the school. These findings may be disseminated across the school and subsequently taken up as a topic for further inquiry involving more participants and thus moving further along the continuum towards extended practitioner inquiry.

TABLE 4.1 The practitioner inquiry spectrum

Collaboration	One-to-one collaboration	)))))))))	A collaboration involving a group or team
Inquiry	Small-scale inquiry into practice	)))))))))	Large-scale inquiry into practice
Context	Local context for practice within the institution	)))))))))	A wider professional context
Criticality	Small-scale question	)))))))))	A broader question with potential for wider application
Evidence	Small-scale processes for evidence collection	)))))))))	Multi-faceted processes for collecting evidence
Interpretation	Simple level of interpretation and analysis of evidence	)))))))))	Complex analysis and interpretation of a well-developed and wide-ranging evidence base
Change/ transformation	Individual change/ transformation	)))))))))	Broader impact
Dissemination	Limited dissemination within the institution	)))))))))	High degree of public dissemination

The eight elements which form the spectrum can be summarised as follows.

Collaboration

The importance of dialogue and collaboration for achieving transformative professional learning has already been discussed in Chapter 2. It is important to also realise that the nature and quality of the collaborative relationship could be affected by issues related to, for example, organisational features, professional roles, power dimensions, policy and legislative frameworks, cultural ethos and community aspects.

Inquiry

Inquiry is essential as a process and a goal to the notion of transformative professional learning employing reflection, dialogue and criticality (see Chapter 2).

Context

The consideration of contextual factors is crucial to any form of practitioner inquiry. Practitioner inquiry is usually undertaken within a particular local context for the benefit/improvement of that context and/or the individuals within it. Contextual factors exist at individual, institutional, national and possibly international levels. It can be useful to investigate the practice of a different professional context in order to gain a sharper perspective and deeper understanding of a more familiar professional context as in the inquiries detailed in Chapter 6.

Criticality

Criticality involves taking a critical approach in order to conduct an inquiry. This approach should raise questions about everyday practice in order to examine it in a more objective way. The questions will consider a specific issue from a number of alternative perspectives. It will also involve the questioning of assumptions and values underpinning systems and practices. Criticality is thinking which is more focused as a result of questioning and evaluation of the different perspectives which this questioning generates.

Whatever the scale of the inquiry being undertaken, a high level of criticality is essential to the questioning process even for questions at a simple level.

Evidence

This is what teachers collect in order to investigate their questions. It may involve any of the following:

- reading of academic, theoretical texts;
- reading of policy and legislative frameworks;
- systematic observations;
- interviews;
- questionnaires;
- quantitative data collection;
- narrative from participants.

Small-scale inquiries are likely to use a more limited range of approaches to evidence collection, whilst practitioner research will employ a range of methods to enable a multi-faceted interpretation of the evidence.

However small-scale the inquiry, ethical considerations still apply to any evidence collected. A useful starting point are the guidelines published by the British Educational Research Association (BERA 2004). It is particularly important to follow ethical guidelines when conducting a practitioner inquiry because of the professional context in which they are being conducted. Denscombe (1998) cites three guiding principles related to ethical issues for researchers. These are:

1. The protection of participants' interests.
2. The avoidance of deception and misrepresentation.
3. The need for the informed consent from participants.

Thus special care must be taken with the way people and institutions are represented within local contexts.

Interpretation

Interpreting the evidence involves revisiting the original question and aim of the inquiry and scrutinising the evidence collected in order to identify themes and patterns related to the original question. This process of focusing and selecting evidence enables the teacher to draw conclusions related to the original question. On a small scale this interpretation will be restricted in scope, maybe to a single theme or aspect within practice. A larger-scale inquiry will result in a more complex process of selection and interpretation from a wider-ranging evidence base. Whatever the scale of the inquiry, it is important that the teacher maintains a degree of criticality throughout the inquiry and continuously reviews any tentative conclusions reached.

Change/transformation

The resulting changes and transformations from the process of inquiry may be at a number of levels. At an individual level this might be a change in an aspect of individual practice such as development of a specific skill or process or an increase in a combination of both knowledge and skill. The inquiry process could also lead to a change in a professional relationship such as a mentoring or coaching relationship. Thus a small-scale inquiry is likely to develop more personal theories for individual use, whilst larger-scale inquiries could impact on more widely established knowledge frameworks.

A larger-scale inquiry might lead to institutional change such as departmental- or school-level change of policy or practice. A practitioner inquiry at the extreme end of the spectrum might lead to a wider social impact, for example on local authority or national policy.

Dissemination

Whatever the scale of the inquiry the outcomes could be disseminated at either a very local level (e.g. one-on-one or within a department/school) or wider across a group of schools within a local authority, or indeed nationally. It is perfectly possible for a small-scale inquiry conducted by one teacher to be disseminated nationally or even internationally at a conference.

How does practitioner inquiry link to mentoring and coaching?

The eight elements of practitioner inquiry can be linked to professional inquiries on any topic. For the purposes of this book we are interested in inquiries which either use the mentoring and coaching collaborative relationship as a platform for investigation into professional practice or inquiries which investigate an aspect of the collaborative mentoring and coaching relationship. We have found the spectrum a useful model for conceptualising the range of possible professional inquiries which could enhance the learning within mentoring and coaching relationships. The model emphasises the centrality of collaboration to the inquiry process. This collaboration enhances this process of inquiry through the use of reflective, critical dialogue within mentoring and coaching relationships.

Illustrations of the collaborative model of professional inquiry can be found in Part II. All the inquiries in Part II demonstrate the potential of mentoring and coaching for individual and institutional development as well as dissemination of the impact of the inquiry at an institutional level and beyond.

PART II
Inquiries

5

Inquiring into the nature of mentoring and coaching through collaboration

Key learning points

- aims of and learning outcomes from a postgraduate course investigating mentoring and coaching in schools;
- the experience of collaboration within the course;
- the critical inquiry approach;
- the impact of the course on professional learning about mentoring and coaching in schools.

This chapter explores mentoring and coaching in schools by examining the outcomes of a collaboration between and by teacher participants taking a postgraduate course on mentoring and coaching in schools. The course was designed to develop participants' professional learning by collaboratively investigating the nature and purposes as well as the processes of mentoring and coaching. The participants were all experienced teachers who had previously acted as mentors for trainee and newly qualified teachers. Central to the course was the use of collaborative critical inquiry (see Chapter 4) in order to deepen the professional learning outcomes, thus allowing for a multi-faceted interpretation and review of individual practices.

Throughout the course the participants engaged in a number of different collaborations in order to investigate the nature of mentoring and coaching and its uses in school settings. These collaborations included participants working:

- as course participants with each other and with course tutors;
- as professional inquirers with school-based mentors, coaches and other staff;
- as professional inquirers with mentors and coaches from other professional contexts;
- with colleagues as mentors and coaches inquiring into their own practice.

These collaborative processes allowed the course participants to set up their own inquiries into mentoring and coaching practices in a range of professional contexts.

The postgraduate course consists of three modules which enable participants to take a collaborative critical inquiry approach to examining the nature of professional learning within mentoring and coaching relationships. Each module allows participants to engage in an increasingly complex level of inquiry (see the practitioner inquiry spectrum in Chapter 4).

The first module sets up the collaborative practitioner inquiry-based approach to professional learning in mentoring and coaching which is used throughout the course. This approach engages the participants in dialogue and critical reflection. Specifically the module investigates the role and place of mentoring and coaching in school contexts. It explores a range of different models of mentoring and coaching and considers issues that affect the mentoring and coaching collaboration such as political and contextual issues. The participants conduct a small-scale inquiry in their local context and disseminate their findings to the course group.

The second module continues the collaborative practitioner inquiry-based approach to professional learning in mentoring and coaching. Specifically it focuses on an examination and analysis of mentoring and coaching in a range of different professional contexts. The participants conduct detailed inquiries which enable them to make comparative analyses of mentoring and coaching practices in different professional contexts in order to make applications to a school context. The participants are able to disseminate their interpretations of findings to a group of people from different professional contexts.

The final module involves a larger-scale practitioner inquiry related to mentoring and coaching practice in participants' own school contexts. In order to carry out the inquiry, participants first undertake a more detailed study of practitioner research processes.

This inquiry is designed to enhance school policy and/or practices and to extend professional learning about mentoring and coaching at both individual and institutional levels. Ensuing dissemination of evidence and analysis enables greater impact at both these levels.

The course had a range of outcomes for the participants which demonstrate how the use of a collaborative critical inquiry-based approach to extending understandings of mentoring and coaching can enhance professional learning. What follows is evidence of these outcomes derived from a number of participants' reflections on the impact of the course.

In these reflections the participants identified a number of features related to the nature and quality of the different collaborations experienced throughout the course. The positive impact of these collaborations on participants' professional learning is demonstrated by the comments in the tables. Table 5.1 shows comments about the nature of teacher participants' various collaborations. Table 5.2 contains comments about the quality of these collaborations. In their comments participants use a variety of terms such as group, community of practice and partnership to refer to their collaborations with each other.

Additionally, participants' reflections on the outcomes of the course revealed the positive impact of adopting a critical inquiry-based approach to mentoring and coaching (see Chapter 4). The key features of this impact are identified and commented on in Table 5.3.

TABLE 5.1 Nature of the collaboration

Feature	Comments
Diversity	'This created a group that had a diverse range of skills, as well as views and opinions'
	'The other members of the group were not known by me prior to the course and as they were different ages to me, taught in different institutions and taught different subjects to me we were able to share diverse experiences and perspectives of the role of mentor in the educational context'
Common interest and commitment to collaboration	'One of the benefits to undertaking the course with a small cohort was the opportunity to work in partnership with like-minded individuals interested in personal growth and professional development'
	'Not since my days as an athlete and brief spells within my role as head of department, had I genuinely experienced a shared vision and work ethic where all participants felt comfortable in their role and the part they had to play in achieving positive outcomes'

Continued overleaf

TABLE 5.1 Continued

Feature	Comments
Group identity	'Although I was keen to extend my skill-set and use this experience to grow both as an individual and professional, I had a genuine urge for all members of the cohort (including the tutors) to excel. This acted as a catalyst for our raised expectations and successful learning outcomes'
	'The collaborations also took the form of an extension from the traditional university seminar, where we could, as a community, explore the issues that were arising in the topics of discussion without pre-judgement or agenda. Rather the community set aside a proportion of time to discuss the larger theoretical and practical difficulties with mentoring and coaching, the merits and inadequacies of previous writing on the subject, and its relation to our own, personal, circumstances'
Flexibility	'The two lecturers also formed part of the group as active learners which facilitated a range of issues to be explored through discussion'
	'A significant amount of mentoring took place in the form of one-to-one tutorials between the teachers and tutors. This would often take the form of looking at the whole person's life at that point to ascertain what could reasonably be done within the deadline, and where suitable time could be found to write the essays and conduct the research'
	'The role of the facilitator is key in ensuring that the extent of the exploration is summarised and is kept relevant to the question. If the group dynamic is managed in the right way, participants have the opportunity to develop not only understanding of abstract knowledge but also enhance a skill-set which lends itself to greater efficiency in the workplace'
Networking	'Although the collaboration was very much directed by the course content, the networking opportunities extended to a wider support role'
	'The guest speakers that came into the sessions acted more as an extension to the community of practice than as experts, though they were indeed experts in their respective fields. They allowed for the community to discuss new approaches to mentoring and coaching, while listening to and analysing the various approaches to the relationships that exist across education, and in the wider public and private sectors'
Modes of communication	'The group was able to collaborate in several ways. First there was an online group set up for the participants to record their views and comments about the topics that arose in the university sessions. This sharing of ideas was useful in helping to form a clearer understanding of the nuances between the distinctions of coaching and co-coaching that I found difficult at the beginning of the course. There was also coaching via email, especially at the time essays were due, that were frequently the questioning techniques used in mentoring to elicit deeper understanding of a given topic or issue. This was probably the single most useful aspect of mentoring and coaching within the community of practice that undertook the course. The discussions that took place online around the various issues allowed me to view theoretical writings in ways I had not considered before, and to listen to different interpretations of the theory'
	'As a group we settled very quickly into being a learning community utilising various means of communication supportively'

TABLE 5.2 Quality of the collaboration

Features	Comments
Supportive of risk taking	'I recall initial concerns . . . it appeared that no-one really knew what to expect or how things would turn out. I feel this uncertainty became the main strength of the group. Not too dissimilar to my experiences with outdoor and adventurous activities, the sense of perceived danger, risk and open-ended exploration led to quicker rates of progress as well as feelings of immense satisfaction'
	'I feel that the process of collaboration has given me the confidence to execute under pressure'
Trust	'. . . the honesty and trust which grew between group members as the course progressed. No hidden agendas, no politics, no tension – despite covering the work of Bourdieu . . . and spending many hours discussing the power struggle which exists in most educational contexts, this was simply null and void from the outset on this course'
	'In operation, it was a dynamic sounding board which allowed contributions to be made, both written and verbal, without fear of failure'
Intellectual challenge	'Full and frank discussion in groups clearly extends thought processes if the context allows it to do so. Crucial to a true collaboration being formed there needs to be critical reflection by all concerned to keep contextual discussion moving forward. If elements of exploration can be added in problem solving scenarios then thinking can be extended beyond normal and expected levels'
	'In-class sessions were often based around specific reading and initially defining the terms 'coaching' and 'mentoring' was crucial in allowing us to formulate our own understanding of what they meant. Here the experience and views of others in the group was especially helpful'

TABLE 5.3 The critical inquiry approach

Feature	Comments
Building on previous professional understanding	'On a personal level, prior to undertaking the course, I had a wide range of experiences and understanding of mentoring and coaching in the schooling context which came in the form of ITT and a variety of NCSL courses. Combined with the practical nature of my specialism, I was able to very quickly grasp the specific nature of mentoring and coaching and apply them to range of situations both within and away from education'
Changes to professional skill, understandings and practice at individual and/or institutional levels	'Despite thirteen years in education, . . . critical thinking and analysis was a necessary part of my self-development and professional growth. On reflection, the introduction to well-established theories which had been alien to me in the past quickly sharpened the mind . . . to critical, independent inquirer'
	'It became clear to me that my own practice of mentoring would have to change if I were to be a more successful mentor and that I could draw on models of mentoring practice that did not relate directly to the world of education'

Continued overleaf

TABLE 5.3 Continued

Feature	Comments
	'The outcome of the course for my own professional development was a clearer understanding, not just of my own practice and how it could be improved, but of a radical rethink in the ways mentoring could be applied to school based professional learning'
	'The final investigation . . . had the most powerful impact on my professional understanding. I conducted an investigation into the factors involved in mentoring student teachers and first year teachers, drawing on my own practice, inquiring if these could be enhanced through the use of technology. This had several mentoring consequences; despite being an experienced mentor myself, I found I was learning new ways of mentoring through the discussions I was having with my mentees about the best ways for them to be mentored'
	'My investigation of coaching within a school context featured my coaching a member of the senior leadership team. This suggested that coaching needn't have a power dynamic that dictates the agenda of the coaching sessions, for I was the party that had the information to share, yet was by far the junior member of staff in this coaching relationship'
Application of theoretical complexities	'One of the most challenging areas was the number of different models of mentoring and coaching that were encountered and understanding the rationale for their formation. Alongside this was the task of trying to see where, when and how they could be implemented and whether or not one model could account for all the things we understood coaching and mentoring to involve'
	'The investigation into how mentoring is formally conducted in other large institutions had a significant impact on my personal understanding, and opinion, of school based mentoring, especially that of mentoring student teachers and those in their first year. By discussing the role of mentoring with a range of people involved in mentoring in their own institutions, either as mentor or mentee, I gained a broader and deeper understanding of, not only the different methods that mentoring could draw on, but the very purpose of mentoring'
	'This approach directed me to testing theory, providing greater consistency, quality and meaningful opportunities for others as a consequence. This has now become something of a model I will take with me as I try to build a shared vision with mentoring and coaching based in the working environment'
Adopting a more critical stance	'I feel that group discussions taught me to speed my process of critical reflection . . . . Evidence to back this would be the early work on module one which involved the analysis of learning models . . . . On the introduction of critical discussion, I started to develop a balanced perspective as to how these models may be applicable to the school context'
	'The tasks allowed exploration of our own experiences and practices but had outcomes that had practical value too. By reflecting on our own institutions and looking into the work of other organizations we were able to use comparative data to draw conclusions or make recommendations'

TABLE 5.3 Continued

Feature	Comments
	'It was also at this point in the course that I truly realised that schools, by design, have significant external power horizons that govern the way in which mentoring relationships exist'
	'The opportunity to push the boundaries and cast a critical eye over the running of educational establishments at all levels of operation allowed me to develop a genuine agenda to raising achievement in a personalised and rational manner'
	'The process of critical enquiry throughout the course kept the foci on the teachers' own experience and practice'
Developing new perspectives for mentoring and coaching practices	'Particularly the issues of power, time, and the on-line/off-line debate could dramatically change the way in which mentoring occurs in schools, and how we develop the less experienced teachers'
	'I later theorised that actually co-coaching was a theoretical impossibility, as coaching determines that one side knows something that the other does not, therefore, at the very least, it is a see-saw of coaching that flips from one side to the other. However the power dynamic within the relationship became, for me, a key feature of the contextual issue that dogs all mentoring and coaching relationships'
	'I firmly believe that this type of enquiry results in generating wider learning opportunities forming, in my opinion, the best form of CPD that can run in schools. It serves to provide not only a critical insight into the contextual issues of schools but provides the platform for those involved to take ownership in a solution driven model. It allows for innovation and creativity in thinking/practice, in turn building motivation which extends beyond the operations of those involved. It serves to engage teachers and students alike'
	'The model would be an increasing cycle of:'
	■ investigation; ■ reflection through coaching and mentoring; ■ increased understanding; ■ sharing of that understanding through co-coaching; ■ a paradigm shift; ■ a new investigation based on an increased understanding of the issues as a whole.
	The model works for each individual but is meant to represent the community as a whole in its search for a definitive model . . . of mentoring and coaching . . . each time the paradigm shift occurs the cycle . . . enlarges as the community draws in more factors and conditions'

This chapter has explored the impact of collaboration and the use of critical inquiry on participants studying a postgraduate course on mentoring and coaching in schools. It is clear from their comments that different individuals gained a variety of specific insights from their experiences of the course, according to their variable prior experience, needs and school contexts. However, the process of collaboration and inquiry provided by the course clearly extended the depth and range of all participants' professional learning.

One of the aspects of the course that participants valued was the work carried out for module 2 investigating mentoring and coaching practices in a range of professional contexts not directly related to schools. They highlighted the usefulness of a comparative approach to inform mentoring and coaching practice for schools. The next chapter will present more detailed accounts of inquiries into different professional contexts, highlighting their relevance to a school context.

Investigation for Chapter 5

Purpose

A small-scale inquiry into personal experiences of collaboration in mentoring and coaching to explore ideas raised in this chapter. Teachers will investigate their own experiences of mentoring and coaching and the use of collaboration.

Action

Identify a specific previous experience of mentoring and/or coaching. Examine the nature and quality of the mentoring and coaching collaboration and record, reflect on and analyse this experience. Table 5.4 is provided to help with this task. When completing the table, refer to the examples of Tables 5.1 and 5.2 which show teachers' comments on the features of a collaboration. It may be necessary to modify the features identified or add further features relevant to the specific experience.

Having examined the mentoring and/or coaching collaboration in this way, a useful step is to compare it with similar investigations undertaken by other colleagues in order to plan further action for change or development.

TABLE 5.4 The nature and quality of the collaboration

Feature	Comments (records, reflections and analysis)
Diversity (differences of status, age, gender, ethnicity, culture etc.)	
Interest in and commitment to collaboration	
Flexibility of roles	
Modes of communication	
Trust	
Attitude to risk-taking	
Challenge (intellectual and practical)	
Other features	

Evaluation of the inquiry

Use Evaluation Templates 1.1 and 1.2 on pp. 13–14 to assess the scale of impact of the collaborative mentoring- and/or coaching-focused inquiry on professional learning for the individual, the institution and the education profession.

6

Inquiring into mentoring and coaching in a range of professional contexts

Key learning points

- inquiring into mentoring and coaching approaches in other professions;
- application of inquiry findings to a school context;
- different professional understandings and uses of mentoring and coaching;
- the relevance of an inquiry-based approach to professional learning.

This chapter shows how two inquiries conducted by teachers into mentoring and coaching collaborations in contexts outside of education provided new perspectives which led to an impact on their professional learning and practice within the education context. The first of these is an inquiry which focuses on a mentoring scheme used by a large publicly funded body in a major city. The second looks at the use of mentoring and coaching by an adult training provider funded to work with the unemployed. These are followed by an inquiry conducted by a visiting tutor into the development of a collaborative mentoring framework for medical consultants. The relevance of all three inquiries for the education context and for teachers' professional learning is considered. The chapter demonstrates the value of gaining new perspectives by inquiring outside the familiar context.

Each inquiry is written by the teacher practitioner who

conducted it in order to provide authentic examples of teacher-led practitioner inquiries into mentoring and coaching practices. In the inquiries the quotations identified as 'Voice' derive from interviews undertaken by the teachers conducting the inquiries.

Inquiry 1

Context

The intended outcome of this inquiry was to see if education (and specifically mentoring for postgraduate certificate in education (PGCE) and newly qualified teacher (NQT) purposes) has anything to learn from other public sector organisations' approach to mentoring. The inquiry focuses on a large publicly funded body with a substantial annual budget and employing a huge workforce (henceforth referred to as 'the organisation').

This organisation's mentoring scheme possesses clear structures and processes, including a Code of Conduct. Those who want to join the programme must seek authorisation from their line manager and must apply to join before being accepted. The programme lasts one year and has been steadily growing since its inception. The mentoring programme is open to all levels of employee. The programme is voluntary, which has a major impact on the implications of who is taking up the challenge of becoming a mentee within the organisation. Though line managers can strongly recommend that employees undertake mentoring, they cannot insist upon it. This leaves the question of how those who need mentoring the most, and therefore may be the most unlikely to take up the challenge, will be encouraged to undertake the process.

One of the factors considered in pairing mentors and mentees is that neither party will have line management responsibilities over the other. In short, the mentee will not be mentored by their boss. However, mentors are expected to be experienced members of the organisation. This is often referred to as 'off-line' mentoring and it is an essential ethos of the organisation. Megginson and Clutterbuck (2005) consider off-line mentoring appropriate because of the difficulty of being open in a professional relationship where one person has authority over the other. Once the mentee is on the programme, the needs of the individual mentee become the contextual factors affecting the process and the outcome.

The organisation also provides a support group responsible for managing and supporting mentors, particularly helping in times of crisis. It appears that the support group does not mentor the mentors, but rather informs those engaged in the programme on best practice and offers mediation to those facing difficulties with their mentoring partnerships. The group provides the training for mentoring and reviews the programme, making periodic evaluations. The group also handles any complaints from the mentors or mentees.

The organisation places a high priority on the development of self-confidence and self-awareness with a primary focus on the skills that enable individuals to operate effectively as leaders and achievers. The organisation is also thinking long-term about succession planning via the mentoring scheme.

The organisation identifies a number of benefits of the mentoring scheme. The first of these is for the mentee. Mentees benefit by having a 'non-threatening learning opportunity that is also a source of guidance, reassurance and strength' (Voice). The relevance for the mentee is the learning journey that will help both their personal and professional life while at the organisation. It is suggested in the organisation's literature that those who have been a mentee are more likely to be promoted (presumably because the mentoring process has equipped the mentee with management skills, particularly reflective and critical thinking). This raises the issue that if the programme is voluntary, those more driven, and therefore more likely to be promoted, are the individuals who will both undertake the mentoring process and be promoted.

The second benefit of the mentoring scheme is for the mentor. Benefits for the mentor are less clear cut; however, the organisation recognises that the scheme offers the chance to share expertise and practise management skills, thereby increasing recognition and expanding horizons.

The third benefit is for the organisation. Certainly the ideas of a more focused workforce and a greater retention of the workforce are shared by the mentors and mentees interviewed during this inquiry. However, in such a vast organisation, the uptake for the programme is still relatively small and it will be years before wide-reaching implications and advantages for the company are seen. It is clear that the organisation values the professional learning of individuals developed through the mentoring process. The inquiry revealed that self-confidence and a greater understanding of one's purpose and job are essential outcomes of the mentoring process. However, as these skills are not assessed in any way by the organisation the specific benefits to the organisation remain unclear.

Process

The process is established by the support group. Meetings must take place every three months, though they can be more frequent. The initial meeting establishes the aims and objectives of the process, as set out by the mentee, and then the relationship plays out according to how the mentor/mentee decides. If things go wrong, the organisation has a clear complaints procedure.

The mentoring process has a clear ethos of a learning journey as the mentoring is conducted on a holistic basis and over a long time-scale. The mentor cannot influence work-related performance indicators or review.

The idea that the mentoring process should be about transformative learning has been endorsed by the findings of this inquiry. It is the clearest indication that the organisation employs an evolutionary mentoring model, as 'evolutionary mentoring [is] an agreed activity between mentor and client, where goals are generated by and for the client [in this case the employee], the process is person-centred and the learning outcome is transformation' (Brockbank and McGill 2006: 75). This contrasts starkly with the mentoring that is often used in education, described as 'functionalist' by Brockbank and McGill where 'a prescribed purpose that may or may not be assented to by the client' (ibid.: 64). This describes perfectly the mentoring partnerships that exist for large numbers of PGCE students and NQTs across the country.

Outcomes and relevance for the school context

There are an obvious number of similarities between the organisation's mentoring programme and the mentoring that takes place in the world of education. The following four similarities are not meant to be an exhaustive list, but offer an insight into how similar the basic premise and rationale for mentoring is between these two different areas within the public sector. In both cases the mentoring process is focused on (a) holistic development of the mentee,

(b) personalised outcomes (c) training for mentors, and (d) a process that is formalised in policy. There remains, however, a tension between the personalised agenda and the constraints of policy. For example, while the outcomes are personalised for PGCE students, there is nevertheless a set of professional standards against which they are judged. For the organisation, the outcomes are entirely chosen by the mentee, meaning that some of the outcomes could focus on an area outside of the mentee's core work objectives or even help them gain the skills to leave the organisation, while PGCE students could not ask to be mentored on anything but meeting the standards required to become a qualified teacher.

The definitive differences are interesting as they can also inform what education might learn from the mentoring process of this organisation. Broadly speaking there are five differences related to the structure and process of mentoring and these are set out in Table 6.1.

One of the most interesting differences is that the organisation's mentoring scheme takes place in a relationship that is exclusively outside of a line management and professional standards structure. Since the relationship is based on a holistic learning journey, the skills being developed are often more general. The organisation is clear that mentoring is a holistic learning journey conducted over a long period of time rather than a process aimed at meeting specific goals in terms of professional competencies within a clearly defined time frame. An implication of using an 'off-line' policy for mentoring as a holistic journey is there can be no 'failure'. If the programme is voluntary, and leaving the programme confers no adverse consequences the concept of failure has no meaning. As the

TABLE 6.1 Differences in the mentoring processes of the organisation and of education

The organisation	Education
Not assessed	Each stage assessed
Meeting infrequent	Regular and frequent meeting
Can leave mentoring with no consequences	Leaving mentoring (PGCE/NQT) means leaving profession
Not allowed within line-management structure	Often mentoring exists within line-management structure
Outcomes are not formalised but fluid	Outcomes are formalised

assessments of the outcomes are taking place within the mentor/ mentee relationships, so success is also being defined by these parties.

If schools were to adopt a more holistic approach a clearer distinction could be made between mentoring and coaching in order to integrate a more holistic professional learning experience with assessment of professional competence against national standards. Thus a mentor for a PGCE trainee could be any experienced member of staff with coaching for specific professional standards being provided in addition by relevant staff members. The organisation's use of quarterly meetings would be impractical in education for PGCE and NQT mentoring as these are year-long courses and developments in the mentee's educational skills are likely to be fast paced, necessitating a more frequent meeting schedule.

If educational mentoring were to consider the holistic needs of the mentee a possible result would be a partial resolution to the potential future shortage of head teachers. The National Professional Qualification for Headship, Leadership Pathways course, and the Fast Track for Headship schemes go some way toward succession planning, but where is the holistic mentoring for succession planning for teachers in their NQT year or as main-scale teachers?

An interesting comparison raised from this inquiry is whether education should only use mentors who have chosen to become mentors. Often educational heads of department assume the responsibility of mentoring as part of their role. The organisation, with its 'off-line' policy and the fact that middle managers are not expected (or forced, directly or subtly) to become mentors, is much more likely to get the best people as mentors, people with drive and passion to be a mentor.

Inquiry 2

Context

The intended outcome of this inquiry was to see if education has anything to learn from the use of coaching and mentoring in an adult training company (henceforth referred to as 'the company') funded to work with the unemployed. The company prepares clients (mentees) for business start-up. It deals with people who have been unemployed for a period of six months or over. The goal is to support entry into self-employment. The process allows a journey to take place which enables mentees to overcome difficulties of a technical and operational nature allowing a concerted move towards self-directed learning. The real essence of the journey, however, allows the mentee to make personal adjustments to their attitudes, ideals and beliefs. This fits with the aims identified by the company's mentors who expressed a desire to 'transform lives' (Voice) enabling mentees to realise solutions of their own accord. The company is subject to Ofsted inspections which have commented on the strong and flexible coaching and mentoring which exists within the company.

In order to explore the values and beliefs and protocols of the company, I conducted interviews with two mentors. The purposes of the interviews were to clarify definitions, identify operational and technical contexts to which the mentees are exposed and finally analyse the process adopted by the mentors to cater for the needs of each individual.

Mentees are required to have been unemployed for a minimum of six months. They often enter the process with extreme issues such as addiction, low self-esteem, financial problems, etc. They are assigned to mentors who are known as business advisors and this inquiry identified some common characteristics in the qualifications of the business advisor/mentor. These are:

- professional accreditation and membership from relevant bodies;
- technical knowledge related to quality standards;
- personal communication skills;
- appropriate professional learning, e.g. an evidence-based portfolio and completion of a required amount of continual professional development.

The two business advisors/mentors interviewed for the inquiry had varying degrees of business experience.

Process

Both business advisors/mentors identified the complex range of roles and skills needed for mentoring. They agreed that they were never 'one person' (Voice) but mentioned the use of a skills set which included adopting the roles of expert, counsellor, mentor, coach, critical friend and a supplier of technical knowledge in a range of disciplines specific to mentee needs. They identified key components of the mentor's role. These were to inform, guide, listen, coach, provide advice, facilitate, bounce ideas (sound-board), brain-storm, collaborate, set goals, provide a holistic approach/client-centred process and use their expertise, knowledge and experience in order to achieve desired outcomes. Both business advisors/mentors felt strongly that the range of personal problems and social issues presented by mentees needed to be addressed early within the mentoring relationship in order to reduce the probability of drop-out.

The mentoring process involves three stages and if certain conditions are met, there is a possibility of extending this process from 18 to 36 months. This combines to make a total of three years, which sets a significant time-scale for all remits of transformative learning to be explored. The same business advisor/mentor acts as the critical source for the duration of the process. The three stages to the process identified are as follows.

Stage 1. Consultation
In the initial phase a one-hour session is held between the mentee and the advisor/mentor. This session focuses on the pros and cons of the mentee's business ideas and the financing of the business. Most importantly any personal, domestic or financial barriers which may prevent start-up are also considered.

Stage 2. Development
If successful in defining the idea and financial structure of the proposed business, mentees undertake an eight-week process where they are asked to develop a business plan. The role of the business advisor/mentor at this point is to act as a critical coach twice weekly. The aim is to ensure that all business operation eventualities are considered prior to moving to the next stage.

Stage 3. Test period
The third and final stage is the test period where mentees can operate their business in safety for a six-month period. Business advisors/mentors meet with the client on a weekly basis during this period and if terms and conditions are correct then a further period of 18 months can be used to support the mentee.

Outcomes and relevance for the school context

One outcome of the process was a clear shift through from coaching to mentoring. What started out as coaching, where business advisors/mentors set out to challenge the client and fast-track their business operation development, became a more holistic mentoring process, where more time was spent questioning the mentee, trying to identify developmental needs. The use of mentoring and coaching leads the mentee on a journey which encompasses personal changes and a formal process to develop self-direction as a self-employed person.

The real strength of this process is the use of mentors' wide-ranging skill set to provide long-term solutions and develop professional learning which runs far deeper than the proposed status upgrade from unemployment to employment.

The school context can draw significant learning from this adult training company's use of mentoring and coaching. Of great importance is the mentor's ability to remain impartial and non-judgmental in face-to-face meetings. Additionally, other skills demonstrated by the business advisors/mentors in this inquiry include emotional intelligence, critical reflection, critical questioning, self-directed learning and improved listening skills. If we, as educators, were able to adopt a similar approach, a more secure environment for personal growth would be achieved, allowing the opportunity to move towards challenging, motivating and supportive professional learning, ultimately producing a more valued, focused and productive staff body. If mentoring and coaching is implemented as part of an institutional ethos the benefits to the individual and the institution are great in terms of productivity, esteem and well-being as well as a widened skills set.

Mentoring and coaching in the school context can learn not only from these successes but also from some of the difficulties identified in this inquiry. The company's mentors seem to provide less intervention if mentees appear to be 'on the right lines' from the outset. In these cases the stages of the business start-up process can be completed without problem, resulting in financial gain for the company. However, it is easy for mentees to pay lip service to the process and hide behind 'spin' designed to convince the business advisor/mentor that they are alert to issues surrounding business start-up, thus minimising and undermining the impact of the process. This may be detrimental in the long term as learning is more superficial and the mentee may not have developed the range of skills needed to cope independently with all the possible difficulties that could be encountered.

* * *

The collaborations exemplified in these two inquiries show differing approaches to structuring mentoring and coaching as processes for professional learning within an institution. However, both inquiries highlight the importance of highly skilled mentoring and coaching which is flexible enough to adapt to the individual needs of mentees. The flexibility and learner-centred approaches found in these two inquiries provide useful lessons for mentoring and coaching in the school context. Thus these insights provide a challenge for schools to ensure the development of a sufficiently individualised approach in mentoring and coaching.

The final inquiry in this chapter traces the implementation of a new approach to developing emerging professionals in a National Health Service (NHS) context through the use of a collaborative approach to mentoring and coaching. This development is of relevance to the school context through its discussion of peer co-coaching and gives further examples of the tensions in professional contexts between the development and assessment of technical competency and the development of professional judgment, confidence and experience. The inquiry also provides a useful model of the use of dialogue, reflection and criticality for professional learning as discussed in Chapter 2.

Inquiry 3

Context

I am a teacher and ex teacher educator, and have worked for the past three years as an advisor in the education department of an NHS postgraduate deanery. My work with hospital clinicians has engaged me in a fascinating new world, with learners, teachers, curricula and educational issues that seem in some respects very different from those I encountered in mainstream education. In other ways, however, there are areas of strong similarity, perhaps most fundamentally in terms of the need to support the development of doctors in training as emerging professionals in contexts of rapid change. In clinical contexts, as in schools, this process is complex, and the qualities that constitute professional competence are vital, but also largely tacit, often evasive and hard to measure. The work I am going to describe here is the development of a co-mentoring scheme for new hospital consultants.

Postgraduate medical education in the UK has seen radical change since the 2005 reforms known generically as Modernising Medical Careers (MMC) (see www.mmc.nhs.uk). Doctors in training emerge from medical colleges and enter what is now a highly structured process of work-based learning, moving through a two-year foundation programme into specialty-specific training lasting for several years. At each stage, there are now clearly defined curricula and expectations, and each trainee works with a clinical supervisor and also an educational supervisor, responsible for their overall development and career progress. The new systems include the use of portfolios and work-based assessments which record the acquisition of clinical and other professional 'competencies'. The increased clarity, structure and accountability are welcomed by many doctors, but within the profession there is also disquiet at the competency-based approach. In my own work I have encountered this disquiet in a number of forms: concern that the new, highly explicit systems instil in junior doctors a form of 'learned helplessness'; that these systems are reductive, failing to describe or develop true professionalism – 'a thousand competencies don't add up to competence' (Voice); and that the new 'run-through' model of training allows less time for development. Rightly or wrongly, there is a strong feeling that newly appointed consultants may lack solid experience and the confidence this brings.

'Consultant to the Power of Two' was a pilot initiative undertaken by the Education Department in our deanery in 2009–10. The idea was to explore ways to support doctors during the transition from specialty training into the role of consultant, specifically in this time of change. Those coming into the role would have received their training under the 'old' arrangements, but would have experienced the turbulence and uncertainty that went along with the introduction of MMC. I worked on the co-mentoring project with a professional coach with particular experience in healthcare settings.

Process

After researching a range of existing mentoring schemes in health-care settings, and regional consultation we decided to pilot a local scheme. We were drawn to a co-mentoring approach for a number of reasons. Co-mentoring is a type of peer mentoring where colleagues work in pairs in order to support and extend each other's professional development. Due to its reciprocal nature, it is of benefit to both participants (see Ragins and Kram 2007). It springs from the close understanding only a peer can give, but the structured and creative nature of co-mentoring means that it is much more than an informal chat. It encourages fresh, independent thinking and we thought it might be a help during the demanding early days of a career as a clinical consultant.

Co-mentoring also has the advantage of being completely separate from any form of assessment or appraisal, and unlike traditional mentoring, does not rely on one colleague's superior knowledge or experience. Instead, it provides a way in which co-mentors can access their own strengths and initiative in order to gain confidence in responding to new challenges. Co-mentors help each other make the most of learning opportunities through supported reflection.

We knew from our initial research that one of the barriers to successful mentoring for hospital doctors has often been the possibility of a deficit model; doctors tend to have impressive records of academic success, and are likely to be suspicious of any implication of weakness. In fact, where they do experience difficulties, an experienced mentor is often put in place as a remedial measure. While we did want to apply some aspects of Egan's 'skilled helper' model (Egan 1990), in order to succeed our scheme needed to steer clear of any suggestion of remediation, or links to appraisal. The scheme's publicity and title, 'Consultant to the Power of Two', put this approach in the foreground. We emphasised the idea of creating a space for reflection outside the complex demands of day-to-day clinical practice, where possibilities, difficulties and strategies could be considered with the help of an interested and informed colleague.

A series of three co-mentor development workshops was offered free of charge to new consultants in our region (two years or less in post) and to final-year specialist registrars. We recruited sixteen participants, representing eight different specialties, from psychiatry to emergency medicine to transplant surgery. The co-mentors came from nine different NHS Trusts, six joined as ready-made pairs, and the rest were partnered either within or across specialties and geographical locations, as far as possible according to their wishes.

The first workshop consisted of a discussion about the participants' prior experience of mentoring, an introduction to the idea of co-mentoring, a brief demonstration and an opportunity for each participant to practise the technique with a partner and observer. We employed Downey's (1999) use of the acronym TGROW as used in 'life coaching' and adapted by Coaching and Mentoring International to mean Topic, Goal, Reality, Options, and Way forward. This provided a structure for co-mentoring sessions between workshops. The 'Goal' refers to a goal for the session – allowing participants to define what they might hope to achieve in the half-hour allocated. In fact, as the scheme progressed we became more interested in the wider possibilities for learning through reflection, rather than focusing specifically on problem solving. We formulated a different, more open-ended structure for use in the second phase of the pilot.

After the first workshop, we learned from the participants that for some, there had been problems in agreeing on where and when to meet. We supplied a contract template and encouraged the co-mentors to negotiate their own agreements in order to keep the partnerships going. In Workshops Two and Three, we built on the approaches introduced at the start, and introduced other techniques such as phone mentoring for those unable to meet regularly in person. Confidentiality was a very real issue, discussed more than once. This raised particularly interesting debate about the nature of professionalism and the boundaries between co-mentoring, membership of a professional group, and friendship. We returned each time to the idea of creating a thinking space, where each mentee was given the space and encouragement to learn through making sense of experience in their own way, and crucially, in their own words. We encouraged the co-mentors to resist the temptation to summarise for their partners. We did not enquire about the content of co-mentoring sessions, but as the group became more relaxed and trusting, conversations started to open up about the stresses and difficulties the participants were experiencing. As we learned more about these we were already formulating ideas for the next phase of the project.

Outcomes and relevance for the school context

We collected monitoring feedback at four stages and in three different formats. This feedback identifies the benefits of co-mentoring between two professionals and these benefits provide evidence of the potential usefulness of co-mentoring for school contexts. The processes for gathering monitoring feedback could also be of value for evaluating mentoring and coaching practices. The four stages for gathering feedback were:

1. Workshop feedback forms completed by participants at the close of each workshop.
2. Phone conversations, text messaging, email and voicemail feedback collected four weeks after Workshop One and Workshop Two.
3. An online anonymous survey circulated to participants eight weeks after the first workshop.
4. An invitation to contribute more detailed narrative accounts of the participants' learning and experiences of co-mentoring.

Though feedback varied depending on individual circumstances and experiences, the majority of comments were very positive and suggested that the participants had valued being part of the scheme.

There was a strong sense that despite the fact that all participants felt extremely pressured in their new roles, and often surprised by the weight of the management responsibilities they were now shouldering in addition to their clinical duties, they found the activity of co-mentoring worthwhile. Voices of participants are included below. Some were explicit about the value they placed on the nature of the process:

> 'It helped with being confident to talk about things I'd not discussed in the past. It worked on a lateral, horizontal level ...'.
>
> 'Everyone has problems that need solving and ... I am not unique; a new Consultant, bumbling through the challenges this brings, and occasionally feeling as if I've not been prepared as well as could have been'.
>
> 'I was surprised at how solutions presented themselves without me having to generate them'.

One participant identified effects that went beyond the co-mentoring partnership itself:

'I went through the technique before the meeting – it was very good. You have to be non-judgemental. I think it will help me in my job situation; now I know how to answer patients' problems.'

For some, though, it remained hard to keep the co-mentoring going between workshops. The time needed to travel and meet the pressing demands of the work were the main difficulties expressed. However, we also sensed that for some participants, the open, non-judgmental approach we were promoting was hard to adopt and even ran counter to the 'differential diagnosis' approach used every day by doctors. In fact, relationships between facts and uncertainties, and the need to pay attention to both of these, are acknowledged as an important part of learning to be a doctor.

Another issue that has emerged is the need to help participants to value their co-mentoring sessions even when they don't go as well as they had hoped. As we watched their progress through the three workshops, we became aware of just how difficult it was proving for some participants to develop the ability to listen well. During the next phase, we aim to incorporate this understanding in the planned workshop discussions. This pilot project is still continuing to be developed.

* * *

Like the previous two inquiries this inquiry emphasises the benefits of mentoring and coaching approaches that value trust and non-judgemental critical reflection on the realities of professional experience.

All three inquiries are able to draw useful comparisons between the professional contexts they investigated in order to enhance their understanding of mentoring and coaching in schools. Each inquiry is characterised by a recognition of the importance of affective factors such as confidence and self-esteem, to professional learning. The inquiries also show how mentoring and coaching structures and collaborations which aim to provide for individual affective factors can find themselves in tension with external professional requirements such as assessment, line management and the development of more technical competences related to the profession. Inquiry 1 reveals mentoring processes which conceptualise a separation between the affective and the more technical aspects of professional learning but are nevertheless concerned to provide mentees with the space to develop trust, confidence and self-esteem away from the pressures of more technical measurements of professional learning. Inquiry 2 shows how the company aims to build the recognition of affective factors into the mentoring process from the outset, alongside advice of a more technical nature. In Inquiry 3, the aim is to promote coherence between affective factors and all aspects of learning by enabling mentees to channel their own intuition in order to continue to learn from experience.

Finally, in all three inquiries the professional learning of the inquirers is enhanced not just by the findings of the inquiries but by ownership of the process of inquiring, collecting and analysing evidence and by disseminating and collaboratively discussing critical reflections on each inquiry. This too has relevance for a school context and has been discussed in Chapter 4.

Investigation for Chapter 6

Purpose

An inquiry into a mentoring and/or coaching collaboration in a context outside of education in order to provide new perspectives on professional learning and practice within the education context.

Action

1. Read the examples of inquiries in this chapter to inform this investigation.
2. Select a suitable professional context outside of education. A suitable context is one which operates mentoring and/or coaching systems and processes which can be compared with teachers' own education context and to which teachers can gain access.
3. Obtain general information about the mentoring and/or coaching scheme, for example by reading or visiting, in order to frame a focused question for the inquiry.
4. Develop a question which aims to explore what the educational context might learn from practice within this different professional context. Ensure this question is manageable within the time and resource limits available.
5. Decide on the evidence required to address the question and plan

the process of collecting data to provide this evidence. The evidence could include the following:

- notes from interviews;
- responses to questionnaires;
- summaries of documentary evidence;
- diary notes;
- notes from observations of practice;
- audio or video recording and photographs.

6. Ensure that ethical guidelines are followed. Those published by the British Educational Research Association (www.bera.ac.uk) are a useful source of information. In summary, consideration must be given to the following:

- obtaining permission from participants;
- explaining the purpose of the inquiry;
- ensuring anonymity of participants;
- sharing information collected with participants for verification;
- being non-intrusive;
- ensuring secure storage of data.

7. Collect the data in line with these guidelines.
8. Analyse the data in order to respond to the inquiry question about lessons to be learned for education about mentoring and coaching practices.
9. Identify and disseminate recommendations.

Evaluation of the inquiry

Use Evaluation Templates 1.1 and 1.2 on pp. 13–14 to assess the scale of impact of the collaborative mentoring- and/or coaching-focused inquiry on professional learning for the individual, the institution and the education profession.

7

Inquiring into one-to-one mentoring and coaching collaborations within the school context

Key learning points

- inquiring into the one-to-one collaboration from the inside – inside the institution and inside the mentoring and coaching collaboration;
- reciprocal learning within the mentoring and coaching collaboration;
- specialist and co-coaching collaborations between experienced teachers;
- specialist coaching as a strategy whilst mentoring a trainee teacher;
- coaching new and experienced senior leaders.

This chapter looks at inquiries conducted within one-to-one mentoring and coaching relationships. These inquiries are notable for the quality of the collaborative approach. In each inquiry the mentor/coach also acts as the inquirer. Each inquiry has a significant (often reciprocal) impact on the individuals concerned as well as different degrees of impact on the institution. They also investigate the nature of mentoring and coaching for professional learning at different stages of teachers' careers ranging form initial training through to support for senior leadership.

The first three inquiries in this chapter give examples of various coaching collaborations. The first one is an inquiry into a collaboration which uses a combination of both specialist and co-coaching approaches to enhance teachers' subject pedagogy through the use of specialist software. The second one is an example of co-coaching to develop a new curriculum area within the school. The third inquiry uses specialist coaching within a mentoring relationship in order to develop a trainee teacher's lesson planning and evaluation.

The two inquiries which examine the use of coaching at senior leadership level show coaching collaborations which allow for focused dialogue and critical reflection aimed at supporting new or changing leadership roles.

Inquiry 1

Context

The context for this inquiry is a small music department in an urban secondary school. The aim of the inquiry was to examine the use of co-coaching and specialist coaching, particularly the notion of reciprocal learning in which both parties can gain from the learning experience and the extent to which coaching can develop a culture of openness and trust. In the inquiry I acted as both coach and inquirer. At the time of the inquiry, I was a new head of department (HOD) who had been teaching for four years, while the coachee was a music teacher with nearly 20 years' experience and as an assistant headteacher (AHT), a member of the school's senior leadership team.

Process

The inquiry focused on developing classroom use of a music-writing software program. This was done in two parts; first a specialist coaching session where I led on the fundamentals of version 3 of the software; and second, where we co-coached each other on the uses and applications of version 5 of the software, in a class setting. In the first (specialist coaching) session issues quickly began to arise around confidence on the part of the AHT, concerned about looking 'foolish' and the power difference was an issue for me coaching someone more senior. These issues were quickly overcome as the level of trust between the two of us built up quickly. The aim of the second (co-coaching) session was summed up best in the words of the AHT; 'to reinforce my own learning, whilst being supported and supporting a colleague'. The second session was conducted with pupils present, this made for a less relaxed session than the first. This changed the dynamic of the coaching relationship as it introduced onlookers with different viewpoints and expectations from the two teachers.

The first session had set up a comfortable relationship which allowed for the level of trust needed to co-coach effectively and we were able to discover together the variations between the two software versions and teach them to the pupils.

The second session allowed for each of us to take control of what we were learning and how to apply this learning to future sessions with pupils. We worked together on the basic functions of the software and how it could be used to produce a score, demonstrating techniques to the pupils, then getting pupils to apply them. As the pupils became more confident they began asking questions about how to produce the more complex aspects of score writing, which we addressed by exploring the software with the pupils, and with each other. However, at several points during the session the AHT felt her confidence waver and at these points she relied on me to coach her and lead the session. After the session we had a period of reflection on what we had learnt and its applications for the future both in terms of the software and our own professional knowledge.

Outcomes

As coach I wanted to use a humanist and relationship-driven style of coaching in the first session similar to Brockbank and McGill's (2006) 'evolutionary approach' (p. 103). We both evaluated the first (specialist coaching) session and the coachee stated in her evaluation that she was made to feel 'valued and in control of my own learning. ... we have a good professional working relationship and I very much admire him'. This shows the trust that had been built up between us. In the second (co-coaching) session I found the trusting and non-judgemental atmosphere highly conducive to effective co-coaching. As the session progressed, I found that the roles between us changed and consequently there was a shift between co- and specialist coaching. This has led to my questioning whether a single (or extended series of) coaching session(s) can remain focused in one type of coaching, and whether the notion of a 'pure' co-coaching or specialist coaching session can exist only in the abstract? As a result of reflecting on theories related to co- and specialist coaching, I developed a better understanding of the skills involved in being a coach (for example being an active listener, agreeing realistic goals, and ensuring that trust is built up).

**

The second inquiry examines a co-coaching relationship between two teachers aiming to develop a new curriculum area within their school. Unlike the first inquiry, the two teachers have similar roles in the school and do not face the same issues relating to power dynamics in terms of seniority and experience, and a co-coaching relationship was constructed whereby each could contribute their own specialist knowledge to the new professional learning.

Inquiry 2

Context

The school in this inquiry is a mixed, urban 11–18-years comprehensive of 1450 pupils. The co-coaching inquiry centred on the introduction, planning and delivery of the Cambridge Latin Course as an after-school lesson which could lead to a GCSE qualification. I was involved in working with a colleague and we acted as co-coaches. We had different subject teaching experience in modern languages and English. We had not previously had the opportunity to work closely together on the same inquiry but selected to work together on this inquiry because we had a shared interest in Latin as linguists and learners.

Process

In response to a request from students for a course in Latin, we decided to raise the issue within the school and explore the possibility of setting up a new course. We decided that although we had different subject teaching skills there was the potential for us to collaborate on the planning and delivery of such a course as we felt we had complementary knowledge and skills. This reflects a key principle of co-coaching that two people elect to work together on a common goal rather than have it imposed upon them.

One teacher researched available courses and subsequently we met to discuss a possible way forward. It was agreed that the Cambridge Latin course offered a workable solution which would involve a mixture of class teaching and independent learning. It was then decided that one of us would focus on delivering the linguistic part of the course, while the other would deliver the background, cultural and historical aspects of the syllabus as well as learning Latin alongside the students. The school was supportive of the proposal to set the course up and run it as an after-school activity. Lessons began in the second half of the autumn term and were held once a week after school, so attendance was voluntary.

Co-coaching is a technique frequently used in education for students in school to help each other in learning situations but is not always considered as a strategy for teachers to work together. When an opportunity arose to initiate a new learning situation, co-coaching seemed the most appropriate approach to facilitate this. As with 'mentoring' and 'coaching' any definition of the term 'co-coaching' is problematic as it can be applied to many different learning situations. This inquiry has drawn on the professional learning gains of co-coaching identified in the CUREE (2004–5) study. This document includes criteria as to who co-coaches are, which seemed to provide an accurate description for this inquiry. The document identifies co-coaches as professional learners who engage in reciprocal learning providing non-judgemental support based on evidence from their own practice.

These criteria do not, however, identify the quality of the relationship which has been fundamental to the success of this inquiry. Brockbank and McGill (2006: Ch. 2) put forward a map of mentoring and coaching approaches which overlays their quadrant model of learning outcomes. The 'evolutionary' area of that map suggests that as a coaching method the evolutionary approach is humanistic and relationship driven, which is certainly an important aspect of this inquiry.

Of all the models of coaching offered by Brockbank and McGill (2006: Ch. 8) the GROW model (Whitmore 1996: 8) is the one that best describes the planning and early stages of the this inquiry. In this inquiry both teachers had interchangeable roles as both coach and coachee, allowing them to reflect on both roles in order to identify what qualities contributed to the inquiry's success. We identified that Rogers' (2004) model of coaching and Egan's (1990) skilled helper model (cited in Brockbank and McGill 2006: Ch. 8) were closest to the way we were working. Both of these models take a more holistic approach where the client has ownership of the goals and Rogers' model in particular begins to explore the quality of coaching relationships.

Outcomes

As co-coaches we developed trust and mutual respect for each other's subject expertise, which meant we felt secure tackling the content of the lessons and were able to share ideas for the delivery of this content. We both brought complementary skills which allowed us to work as a supportive 'double-act' in the classroom. As a result the students also felt confident and comfortable and felt that they had some ownership of this learning situation. The co-coaching relationship in delivering the course was strong, allowing for spontaneity and creativity; uncertainties were discussed in front of students and any difficulty encountered with the lesson delivery resulted in supportive interventions from either teacher. The fact that both teachers were also seen as learners added to the supportive atmosphere.

The outcomes of the inquiry were interesting and beneficial in unexpected ways. Collaborative learning evolved for students and teachers as a result of the teacher collaboration which occurred through co-coaching, rather than through teacher-led activities. The teachers were able to respond to requests to explore areas in more depth, thus extending both subject knowledge and professional learning.

The co-coaching relationship allowed us to take pedagogical risks in the way we approached the students' learning. This has encouraged the students to have the confidence to do the same with their own learning, which has the potential for transformational learning. The inquiry has also highlighted the motivational power of self-selection and ownership of the learning. An added bonus has been the sheer enjoyment of sharing a learning experience through the co-coaching relationship. As the course continues it will be interesting to see how the co-coaching relationship develops and whether the coaching model changes or develops into something else. It has also been revealing to see how different models of mentoring and coaching have a resonance for the work of schools and this leads me to consider what we in education have to contribute to the notions of co-coaching in other areas of work.

* * *

The third inquiry examines a mentor's work with a trainee teacher using a specialist coaching approach to develop a specific aspect of pedagogical practice.

Inquiry 3

Context

The aim of this inquiry is to enhance the teaching and learning of a trainee teacher on a first training placement. It took place in an urban comprehensive school with a population of approximately 1450 students. The trainee teacher was placed in a department which had eight members of staff consisting of two teachers new to the profession, one second-year teacher and the other teachers having between 5 and 35 years' experience.

The inquiry focused on specialist coaching as it used a clearly structured and sustained process to focus on the specific needs of the trainee teacher. It was also anticipated that by briefing the department on the progress of the inquiry, there was scope to develop coaching skills that could have a wider impact across the department.

I, as head of department (HOD), worked in collaboration with the trainee teacher (TT) to carry out this inquiry. I had previously undertaken a training course in mentoring and coaching and undertook this inquiry as a follow-on to the training course. I was new to my role as HOD and was open-minded to the training process and keen to lead the student into the strongest possible position to not only enter the profession but also build a successful career. I felt that a meaningful induction with the student would enhance the process. Systems and protocol for observations and weekly meeting slots were already in place.

Process

The model of specialist coaching used was acquired during a mentors' training course at a local university. The model employed a sequence of four lessons where specialist coaching was used to develop the TT's practice in an identified area of professional learning. We identified the quality of lesson planning and its impact on teaching as a development need.

At the start of the process the TT's delivery of lessons was slow in pace and not sufficiently related to success criteria to meet professional standards. Although his practical demonstrations were of a good standard, his planning led to 'hit and miss' experiences in the classroom as the learners did not fully understand the direction of the lesson and the expectations required. There were also problems identified with the middle and end of lesson activities which raised a range of teaching and learning issues. Of main concern was the tendency of the TT to 'chase the lesson' in an effort to get through all prepared activities, limiting the quality of work undertaken.

To address these issues we arranged for four lessons to be the focus of specialist coaching, in which I as HOD (the coach) and the TT (the coachee) alternated roles as shown in Table 7.1.

TABLE 7.1 Roles taken by HOD and TT in lessons

Sequence	Planning	Teaching	Observed
Lesson 1	HOD	HOD	TT
Lesson 2	TT and HOD	HOD	TT
Lesson 3	TT and HOD	TT	HOD
Lesson 4	TT	TT	HOD

Approximately 30–45 minutes were spent on planning each lesson including developing appropriate resources. Each session was concluded with a written account or verbal debrief between the HOD and TT which facilitated the planning of the next lesson. This took into account the appropriateness of each activity to impact on the quality of teaching/learning.

Outcome

The first indication that the specialist coaching would be a success was when the TT began diagnosing his own development needs.

My use of focused questioning at all stages provided a structure to develop the learning of the TT. It served to direct thinking and produced a foundation for significant changes to occur in the short space of time provided by the specialist coaching inquiry. The initial lessons where the planning and teaching focus was clearly on me as HOD provided opportunities for the modelling of desired outcomes in a range of teaching and learning practices both in and outside of the classroom. As an experienced practitioner I was able to illustrate the fine balance needed in the classroom to impact on the learning of all students.

Although time consuming, the benefits of the specialist coaching inquiry were clear for all to see. Following the four lessons, the TT displayed increased independence and had the confidence to plan and innovate in the classroom. The developments identified by the TT were significant. They included personal growth (confidence, self-esteem and presence in the classroom) and professional development such as subject-specific understanding, the way assessment was used to monitor progress, and linking tasks to pupils' needs.

My own perception of the outcomes of the specialist coaching approach is that although the personal growth of the TT was clear, the professional growth was equally evident. The use of questioning in directing thought processes proved to be a valuable tool to enhance the TT's professional learning. The TT developed the ability to identify the impact of his actions. Also by developing methods of reflection prior to and after lessons he appeared to gain control of his working environment. His teaching interventions eased the transitions between the planned activities. Additionally, more time was being spent on the task due to the engaging nature of planned activities.

The specialist coaching sequence of lessons was designed to work within a restricted period of time; however, the success achieved was consolidated in the following weeks, ensuring continued professional development. It was a positive experience for both myself and the TT. I recommended the practice to be used by other teachers in the department working with this TT.

In conclusion, my inquiry into the use of specialist coaching led to transformational learning not only for the TT, but also for myself and my department. It served to facilitate pedagogical discussion within the department, which had been minimal prior to the inquiry. As HOD it became clear that if I was able to embed the use of mentoring and coaching into the daily management of a department, wider benefits to professional development could be achieved. However, at present I feel it is easier to guide learning in the formative years of teachers than with established teachers as new and trainee teachers tend to be more open-minded and willing to work in collaboration in order to progress.

* * *

The last inquiry is conducted by a professional education coach working for a company that specialises in providing personal performance coaching for senior school leaders. The following background information to the coaching company is provided by the inquirer.

The company seeks to supplement the school improvement support provided by local authorities. Senior school leaders, particularly heads, are in positions where their lives, behaviours, words, actions and relationships are on constant public display and as a result they have to learn how to manage both their private and public personas in a manner that enables them to maintain high levels of authenticity and a deep connection with their core values. When faced with challenging circumstances, which often arise on a daily basis, senior school leaders will normally respond automatically to these situations with perceived expertise and aplomb. Responding to stress, responding to crises, small and large that are not a part of the planned daily routine, soon become an accepted part of a school leader's daily life. However, left unchecked, and without time to reflect on causes, impact and consequences of actions taken, these automatic behaviours can result in leaders becoming disconnected from themselves and in extreme cases disconnected at various levels with those that they lead.

The question arises, 'With whom can the senior school leader have that conversation that simply allows him/her to breathe?'. Such a conversation would allow the individual to gain a deeper level of self awareness in order to link personal and professional understandings to become a congruent and effective leader. This is not an area that school advisors, consultants etc are trained in, but if we are to have effective schools, schools in which both children and staff fulfill their potential, then there have to be systems in place that facilitate school leaders' ability to reflect in an open and honest manner on their leadership.

Thus the company's work with school leaders takes an approach to coaching that is rooted in enabling individuals to develop heightened levels of self awareness and understanding, believing that increased understanding of self, leads to effective leadership. A central tenet of the coaching relationship relies on the coach's belief that if an individual can connect with his/her values and understand the role that they play in their lives; then they are more likely to experience a deeper sense of congruence between their public and private selves and fulfillment in their professional role.

Inquiry 4

The following inquiry provides two illustrations of how the above coaching principles have been used to support a newly appointed secondary deputy headteacher and an experienced headteacher taking on a wider role as a head of two schools. The names of the individuals have been changed to ensure compliance with ethical standards.

1. Newly appointed secondary deputy headteacher

Context

The coachee, Leon, works in a small, urban, secondary church school. Coaching was offered to him as part of the local authority's support programme for new senior appointments. The purpose of the coaching was to provide Leon with a non-judgemental, confidential and private space in which he could, at regular intervals throughout the school year, reflect on his new role and create meaning and understanding for himself of his new leadership experiences, challenges and successes.

Process

The coaching sessions took place once a half-term and were two hours in length; six sessions were held during the academic year. The first session set out the parameters in terms of purpose, timings, location, roles and responsibilities and expected behaviours. This formal contracting of the coaching relationship clarified the differences between this relationship and the role of a School Improvement Partner (SIP) or expert consultant.

The structure of the sessions followed Downey's (1999) use of the TGROW (Topic, Goal, Reality, Options, Will/Wrap-up) acronym together with the stages identified in Egan's (1990) skilled helper model (see Chapter 3, p. 39) Thus a space was created for Leon where he could talk about the past in order to prepare for the future. At the beginning of the coaching relationship there was a need for Leon to tell the story of his journey into leadership, the highs and the lows and the impact that they had had upon him. Egan (1990) recognises that the importance of 'helping clients to tell their stories should not be underestimated.... A story that is brought out into the open is the starting point for possible constructive change' (p. 78). As Leon said in his reflection, 'My experience previously had been such a mixed bag. I needed to work through it, to gain a better understanding and to be able to start again'.

Some schools of coaching shy away from looking into the past, and for good reason. Coaches are not counsellors, and our work with clients is not about dwelling on the past in order to heal inner emotional pain or conflict. Thus in establishing the coaching relationship it is important that the boundaries of the coaching relationship are set, so that both coach and coachee know that where the past is considered it is with the clear purpose and intention of bringing understanding to the individual of where they are now and empowering them to learn from the past and take confident steps into the future.

Leon always set the agenda for the sessions. In a coaching relationship this is very important. Frequently external support visits to a senior leader come with a set agenda which may not be fully owned by the school leader. Although a set agenda may be appropriate for some purposes, it is not appropriate for developing a non-judgemental coaching relationship. In this inquiry the coach has no personal agenda other than to be fully present for the coachee. Thus the relationship that developed between coach and coachee was built upon trust and mutual respect and understanding, illustrated by Leon's comment, 'Trust is the most intimate 1:1 dialogue with another professional colleague; which is absolutely confidential and non-judgemental. Trust allows you to share things and talk through feelings and emotions, knowing that they are with you to support you'.

The coach was able to gain insight into Leon's frame of reference, values and key motivators, blind spots, conflicts and questions not previously shared with others. This enabled the coach to identify what needed to be strengthened, challenged and flexed in order to assist forward movement in his new role, and enabled the coachee to set meaningful goals for development connected to his values and anchored in his sense of purpose and direction. Subsequent coaching sessions focused on:

- Further identifying and exploring core values, related behaviours and their impact.
- Leon's leadership vision and how he wished this to transpire in his new role.
- Leading and managing others in a manner congruent to his beliefs and core values.

Each session concluded with a review and identification of key learning points from the session and steps that Leon identified that he would take in between sessions, to ground his learning and development and ensure continued personal and professional growth.

Outcomes

Coachee

Leon described his experience of coaching as an 'enjoyable, thought provoking process that took me from where I was previously to where I am now'. The inquirer identified Leon's increased confidence as a new leader: coaching provided Leon with the space to realise that past negative experiences did not have to be carried over into his new role. He could indeed learn from them, draw increased wisdom and understanding from what he had previously experienced and in so doing move on confidently and with a high degree of self-assurance.

Coaching enabled Leon to enter his new role with a deep level of integrity and connection to his core values. Through coaching Leon was able to reflect and ask 'why' and 'what' questions of himself, to search for answers and share his solutions with his coach. Leon became aware of just how intrinsically linked his behaviours were to his values and how they had shaped his personal leadership vision:

> My ethos and values where laid naked and explicit. I was able to clearly articulate my values, ethos and vision and identify the roots of things that are founded in me as a leader. I have been able to model and express what I believe in.
>
> (Leon)

Leon, like all leaders, needed a space where he could 'top up' his reservoirs of hope, resilience and optimism as the differing expectations of his new post were high. There were the external pressures of his staff and also the often much harsher and higher expectations that he set for himself. Leon found that coaching enabled him 'to get better at being honest with myself and by being honest with myself I developed greater resilience'. Leon learnt how to mediate between his personal expectations and those of others and in so doing operate from a place where he was able to effectively manage the demands of his new role.

Coach

The process of coaching Leon revealed a number of key learning points for the inquirer to bear in mind when coaching new leaders in future. These are as follows:

1. A space needs to be created which facilitates the new leader telling his/her leadership journey. The telling of the story helps the coach to understand the client's internal frame of reference; what has shaped their personal leadership vision and whether there are any parts of their story that will act as supports for their new role.
2. New leaders need to be supported in clarifying their personal values and making connections between them and their behaviours as a leader. By doing so, the coach helps the individual to identify how his/her values can keep them anchored when faced with the challenges and demands of a new role.
3. The new leader needs to be supported to create a very clear vision of him/herself in a new position. It is likely that a new leader will have observed a range of both effective and ineffective

leadership practices. In order for the new leader to lead with authenticity and confidence s/he must be able to distil what s/he has learnt from these observations and use it to create a unique image of successful leadership.

4. An effective coach helps the new leader to identify strengths and then to see how they can be used as tools for overcoming blind spots and areas for development. In addition, they help the individual to see that any mistakes made are opportunities for learning, which if given the right support, do not need to be feared.

2. Experienced headteacher taking on a new role

Context

The coachee, Shona, works in an urban primary church school. Shona was in the fourteenth year of her career when the coaching relationship started. She was a very successful headteacher whose leadership skills and qualities were widely recognised by her colleagues and local authority. Shona was asked to become the head of another school, an arrangement whereby she would work collaboratively with the governors and teachers of another local primary school, which was without a headteacher, to help develop successful strategies for moving the school forward. This arrangement was in addition to being head of her own school. The coaching support that Shona needed was not related to the operational and structural changes that were required to make this initiative a success, but rather to do with the support required to help her make sense of the unexpected personal transitions that the change in her role brought about. She needed to explore ways to balance the personal and professional demands of her new role and manage the change in professional relationships and self-perception.

Process

The coaching sessions followed Downey's (1999) TGROW model complemented by the coach's knowledge of the four stages of

Kolb's (1984) experiential learning cycle (see Chapter 2, p. 21) and this inquiry is discussed in relation to these two models.

Stage 1. Concrete experience
Shona reflected on the experience of being a head of two schools and the reality of managing the personal and professional transitions that arose as a result.

Stage 2. Reflective observation
When an individual is engaged in new learning, the experience will have an impact at both an emotional and a rational level, resulting in the individual being left with a range of feelings and thoughts about the experience. Individuals need to be given opportunities to reflect on what they have experienced to ensure that new and perhaps more desirable outcomes can be achieved in future. Often, in the busy life of a headteacher, this reflection does not happen and individuals find themselves in a cycle where old behaviours continue to produce the same, sometimes disappointing results. At a subconscious level the individual knows something is not right. They experience a certain discomfort or disconnection from their role and from other people. Thus reflective observation allows the individual to step outside of the situation, reflect as an observer on what they have experienced and come to terms with their feelings about the event/situation.

It is at this stage in the learning cycle that a number of key coaching questions come into play as the coach works with the client to help/him her to gain a greater understanding and as complete a picture as possible about what they have experienced.

Thus, in coaching Shona, questions were asked that enabled her to think through her current reality of managing two schools and what this meant for her on a personal level. The types of questions that were asked at this stage were:

- What expectations did you have of your new role?
- How have your expectations changed?
- What has this experience meant for you?
- How have others responded to your change in role and how have you responded to them?
- What have been the key areas of learning for you?
- What have you learnt about yourself personally?
- What impact has this change in role had upon you?

These questions guided Shona's reflections and enabled her to achieve a higher level of discernment and to view the experience through another lens; a lens that enabled her to see events more clearly and plot a clearer pathway forward for both personal and professional success.

Stage 3. Abstract conceptualisation

This is the stage within Kolb's (1984) cycle where the learner is invited to draw conclusions from his/her reflections and identify what the experience has taught them. Where the experience has involved others they are encouraged to 'theorise' on not only what they have learnt about themselves, but also what they have learnt about others and how this new knowledge can be used to inform future decisions. Within coaching this can often be the 'Aha!' or light-bulb moment for the client. It is the stage at which Shona came to realise that she did indeed have the answers to issues and problems. It is the stage when Shona also realised she could change her behaviours.

Stage 4. Active experimentation

Kolb's (1984) model is cyclical. Therefore once the individual moves to active experimentation and starts to try and test out new behaviours, then he or she moves once again into stage 1, the experiencing phase. This creates a continual process of reflection and as the individual experiences a number of iterations of the cycle, s/he becomes more open to change and the opportunities for self-reflection and development that can be derived from being placed in new situations. This process can be seen in the coachee outcomes below.

Outcomes

Coachee

The key coaching outcomes for Shona provide an acute illustration of the unique supporting role that coaching can have in helping the busy school leader maintain high levels of both personal and professional effectiveness. The two key coaching outcomes for Shona related to:

1. *Maintaining a healthy work–life balance.* Like many head-teachers, Shona had got used to putting the needs of others first.

She had become used to giving on a grand scale and putting her needs last, without paying due attention to the imbalance this was creating in her life as a whole. Coaching enabled Shona to see that investing time in herself, paying attention to the things that renewed and re-energised her, was an essential part of her life's journey, if she was to be fully effective and fulfilled in her role as a leader. She stated:

> Coaching came at a time when I was incredibly tired and made me think how I use my energy. For years I had been doing what I do, not looking after myself – mentally, emotionally and spiritually. I had learnt to ignore things that had a negative impact upon me.

2. *Developing greater self-awareness.* On another level, coaching also enabled Shona to understand herself better. She came to a greater understanding of her personal style of leadership and its impact upon herself and those that she managed. Developing a greater understanding of who she was as a leader also enabled Shona to recognise that some parts of her leadership repertoire were rooted in childhood experiences and to question whether these vestiges of the past still served her well as a school leader. Shona used the analogy of a suitcase to help herself understand the factors that had influenced her as a leader. She described the suitcase as something of value that had been given to her by her parents when she was a child and which she had carried with her through her professional life. Coaching helped her recognise that the suitcase had became too heavy to carry around. Inspection of the suitcase's contents revealed that unbeknown to Shona her parents had placed items in the suitcase to help her understand how to manage conflict and to deal with challenging behaviours. Until now the suitcase and its contents had served Shona relatively well but this new experience of leading two schools revealed the shortcomings of some of the suitcase's contents. Shona realised that she needed the 'courage to stop doubting' herself and to re-inspect the suitcase's contents and make a decision about what she wanted to keep and what she wanted to throw away. Shona stated, 'Coaching helped me to see my role as a headteacher and to realise the areas of myself that I needed to develop. . . . I needed to become a bit more assertive at times'.

Coaching enabled Shona to understand the often complex inter- and intra-personal dynamics that leaders are faced with when dealing with change. She was able to develop new ways of thinking, being and doing. It was the start of a journey that led to new and heightened levels of self-discovery and awareness. She stated:

> Coaching far exceeded my expectations. Somehow you managed to draw out of me answers to the questions that I had in my head and I was able to rationalise what was going on across the two schools ... what you did was, you gave me time and space to find myself, I have come out a better person.

Coach

The coach's facilitation of Shona's profound learning experience revealed the need to engage coachees in discussion and dialogue which leads to greater levels of self-awareness. To do this coaches must possess the personal attributes and tools that will enable their coachees to feel both psychologically and emotionally safe. It is not an easy task for any school leader to drop their public face and to reveal to another their hopes and triumphs, as well as their fears and insecurities. If a coach is committed to helping an individual achieve their best, uncover blind spots and overcome personal barriers to success, then it is important that s/he recognises that coaching is not a superficial relationship. In the context of support for school leaders, it is probably the most intimate relationship that a school leader will ever have with a fellow professional.

This experience of coaching highlighted the importance of building rapport and trust and being non-judgemental. The coach has to create a space where the individual knows endless possibilities can be explored and discussed, and the coach is a trusted confidant. As Shona said:

> If trust hadn't been there, I wouldn't have opened up. I would have gone through the motions. The situation that I was in really took the rug from underneath me. I really needed to be able to open up, so that I could make sense of it all and learn to be myself.

In conclusion, all the inquiries in this chapter report examples of successful collaborations within mentoring and coaching relationships. The components of successful professional learning identified in Chapter 2 can be found in these inquiries. All inquiries rely on reflection, dialogue and criticality in order to advance reciprocal professional learning. The metaphor of mentoring and coaching as a learning platform proposed in Chapter 2 is evident in these inquiries, which all show the importance and impact of creating a space for developing professional learning at different stages of a teacher's career. The inquiries in this chapter also demonstrate the impact of approaching the mentoring and coaching process as a focused collaborative inquiry into aspects of professional learning.

Investigation for Chapter 7

Purpose

To construct an inquiry focused on a specific professional learning issue which uses a one-to-one mentoring and/or coaching collaboration within the school context.

Action

1. Read the examples of inquiries in this chapter to inform this investigation.
2. Select a suitable professional learning issue as the focus for the inquiry as well as the mentoring and/or coaching collaborative partner. This partner may be from an already established mentoring and/or coaching relationship or you may wish to set up a new collaboration.
3. Develop a question which aims to explore the professional learning issue in a way which ensures that findings will be relevant to this specific local collaboration. Ensure this question is manageable within the time and resource limits available.
4. Agree the structure and modes of communication for the collaboration (e.g. frequency and timings of meetings, face-to-face or electronic communication).
5. Decide on the evidence required to address the question and plan the process of collecting data to provide this evidence. The evidence could include the following:

- notes from interviews;
- responses to questionnaires;
- summaries of documentary evidence;
- diary notes;
- notes from observations of practice;
- audio or video recording and photographs.

6. Develop a process for the inquiry which will allow for appropriate evidence to be collected. Look at Inquiry 3 for an example of a process which uses a clear structure of observation and feedback.
7. Ensure that ethical guidelines are followed. Those published by the British Educational Research Association (www.bera.ac.uk) are a useful source of information. In summary, consideration must be given to the following:

- obtaining permission from participants;
- explaining the purpose of the inquiry;
- ensuring anonymity of participants;
- sharing information collected with participants for verification;
- being non-intrusive;
- ensuring secure storage of data.

8. Collect the data in line with these guidelines.
9. Analyse the data in order to address the professional learning issue investigated by the inquiry question.
10. Discuss this analysis within the mentoring and/or coaching collaboration to identify solutions and recommendations. Disseminate these as appropriate within and beyond the local context.

Evaluation of the inquiry

Use Evaluation Templates 1.1 and 1.2 on pp. 13–14 to assess the scale of impact of the collaborative mentoring- and/or coaching-focused inquiry on professional learning for the individual, the institution and the education profession.

8

Inquiring into wider mentoring and coaching collaborations within the school context

Key learning points

- developing larger-scale inquiries and processes for groups and teams of school professionals;
- developing new systems and approaches for mentoring and/ or coaching;
- the potential of mentoring and coaching for effecting institutional change.

While Chapters 6 and 7 have been concerned with examining the nature and use of mentoring and coaching in a variety of contexts, the inquiries in this chapter are larger-scale inquiries aimed at developing new mentoring and coaching practices in secondary schools. These new practices are designed to have an impact at an institutional level. The inquiries involve collaborations between the inquirer and different teams of teachers rather than focusing on one-to-one collaborations. While the inquiries in previous chapters can be seen to contain elements of the practitioner inquiry spectrum described and illustrated in Chapter 4 and could easily be adapted or added to in relation to the spectrum, they occur largely at the small-scale inquiry end of the spectrum. The inquiries in this chapter illustrate all eight elements of the spectrum and contain the elements from the spectrum associated with larger-scale practitioner inquiries. Thus they have a wider dissemination and hence a greater impact at both individual and institutional levels.

The first inquiry investigates the impact of using electronic communication between a mentor and two mentees in the early stages of their teaching careers. The second inquiry examines the impact of developing a peer mentoring support system for aspiring heads of department. The third inquiry investigates the implementation of a new mentoring programme for a senior leadership team.

Inquiry 1

This inquiry looks at the question 'Can the mentoring process be enhanced by the use of technology between a mentor and two mentees?'.

Context

The school in the inquiry is a small urban comprehensive school. The mentor (and inquirer) is a head of department who has been mentoring trainee and newly qualified teachers (NQTs) for around four years. Subject mentoring takes place in scheduled face-to-face meetings which are weekly for trainee teachers and fortnightly for NQTs, but in reality, the scheduled times for the meetings are often subsumed by other things. This means that a significant proportion of mentoring actually takes place in a series of short, informal discussions during the week. For trainee teachers almost every conversation becomes a mentoring dialogue about issues such as lesson observations of the trainee teacher or the mentor, lesson planning, subject knowledge and the working of the school. Additional mentoring is provided in the school to ensure successful assessment and qualification of the trainee teacher and the NQT. The NQT felt that she was not receiving enough mentoring to effectively improve her teaching and this, coupled with the *ad hoc* nature of the mentoring, provided for the trainee teacher and the mentor's concerns about time management instigated this inquiry.

Process

The inquirer took a six-week period to investigate how technology could be used to enhance the mentoring process and chose to focus on the use of two forms of technology, email and text messaging, whilst keeping face-to-face meetings as a third mode of communication. The mentees and mentor exchanged mobile numbers and agreed that they would use the school-based email system. They then explored and agreed the ground rules; either mentee could text or email the mentor with a problem or issue which could then be responded to in any way or time available. Meanwhile, the mentor could pose a problem or question by text or email, or during a face-to-face meeting, but then ask the mentees to respond in a mode of the mentor's choosing. The final rule agreed related to time constraints; the mentor was initially concerned about the issue of privacy, and so wanted to seek to provide the best opportunity for the mentee to access mentoring when needed, whilst balancing this with ensuring that the mentor was not continuously disturbed by the mentee. Therefore the mentor told both mentees that they were not allowed to send text (or email – though due to the asynchronous nature of email this was an artificial barrier) after 7 p.m., or at all on a Sunday. After three weeks of restricted communication time the conditions were changed and this time restriction was removed. This was done for two reasons; first to see if an unrestricted access to mentor's support actually made a difference, and second, to see if by allowing unrestricted access, the privacy of the mentor was invaded to an unacceptable level.

The six-week period of the inquiry covered Easter holidays and the GCSE coursework deadline period. During the Easter holidays, the mentoring continued, often asynchronously through email, or by text that was responded to later. The fifth week covered the GCSE coursework deadline period, which resulted in the mentor and both mentees each working in school for approximately 70 hours. The effect of these breaks in routine was the inconsistent use of technology at certain points, mainly due to the frequency of face to face communication during the coursework period.

For the purposes of the analysis the inquirer categorised the use of technology modes into time taken, generation and nature of response, nature and scope of the question posed (e.g. a question requiring a focused answer using specialist coaching). The inquirer plotted the number of instances technology was used during each week of the investigation.

Outcomes

The impact of this inquiry on the mentoring relationships in the school was significant. It was found that face-to-face meetings could not be completely dispensed with, nor would this be desirable. A constant finding was that although technology enhanced the face-to-face meetings, a lot of the deeper mentoring processes of questioning, reflection and learning still took place on a face-to-face basis. This allowed for the nuances of body language and tone that generated open and probing dialogue. It was also found that the majority of text messages dealt with individual issues and problems, relating more to specialist coaching than to mentoring. However, text messages sent prior to a face-to-face meeting were able to prompt deeper, more reflective questions to the mentees, and could be responded to in an email as a way of opening a dialogue which took a more holistic approach. In fact, texting was most suited to specialist coaching, while email leant itself to deeper level mentoring. This is not a great surprise, for email is a more suitable medium than text messaging for a considered, reflective response to a question or issue posed by the mentor, or a thoughtful elaboration of a point the mentor wants the mentee to understand.

The most interesting finding was that while face-to-face meetings are able to provide a blend of mentoring and specialist coaching (sometimes shifting from one to the other in a single meeting), the electronic communications used in this inquiry seemed to adhere more rigidly to a specific form of mentoring or coaching. For example a significant number of the text message interactions were a form of specialist coaching, as a lot of the texting dealt with specific questions and the nature of texting appears to lend itself to coaching of this kind. Although the mentor was able to use text messaging to provoke deep mentoring with questions like 'what kind of teacher do you want to be?', the answers always came back at a later date in the more discursive form of email or, more likely, at the face-to-face meeting.

The amount of data collected during the inquiry was limited as a result of disruptions to routine affecting the use of technology. However, the inquiry did pose a series of questions which suggest that the use of electronic communication for mentoring and coaching can be problematic as well as useful.

The first of these raises the issue of what happens when communications are lost in the ether. Texts are easily deleted; emails can be deleted accidentally, and both forms of communication are open to misinterpretation. However, given the finding that texts best suit short question-and-answer interactions such as those found in the specialist coaching interactions in this inquiry, perhaps the transient nature of texts is not a significant issue. Second, what happens when technology does not work? A simple power cut can keep either mentor or mentee offline for hours. A mentor that spends a weekend in the country may have no mobile reception and so may not be aware of incoming texts. Third, the intrusive nature of technology, mobile texts and calls late at night or at weekend, or indeed just outside of work hours, can have a claustrophobic effect on the mentor. If a mentor does not limit the time available for mentees, but allows them open access to mentoring when they need it, there is a lack of privacy for the mentor.

Overall the success of this inquiry was its potential for changing the nature of mentoring within the school context, providing evidence of successful mentoring and coaching exchanges which can operate both independently of and in support of face-to-face communications. Additionally, the initial rationale for inquiry, the problem of time management, was resolved for both mentees and the mentor. As a result of the inquiry a significant amount of professional learning took place. The mentor experienced a shift in understanding of how mentoring relationships could take place and how and why technology can enhance those relationships.

Inquiry 2

This inquiry asks 'How can the development of peer mentoring support the role of second-in-charge of a subject department?'.

Context

The inquiry was undertaken in a large urban comprehensive school. A group of deputy heads of department, including some newly appointed to the role, was selected as the sample group. The purpose of this inquiry was to set up and investigate the effectiveness of a new peer-coaching model as a professional development tool for deputy heads of department. It also focused on successful ways of facilitating peer-coaching in order to produce a model which can be replicated across the school. The peer-coaching model was designed to support the deputy heads in identifying problems, developing collaborative approaches and effective management and leadership techniques for their role. The inquiry was led by an experienced head of department, referred to as the lead coach.

Process

The new peer-coaching model was developed around a structured process centred on dialogue and discussion. The process used questionnaires, interviews and peer group meetings (known as a learning set) to guide the participants in understanding the nature of their role. The process involved the following components:

1. interviews and questionnaires;
2. learning-set meetings;
3. an inquiry task.

1. Interviews and questionnaires
Prior to learning-set meetings, a 30–45-minute interview and questionnaire was conducted with each participant asked to identify perceived issues relevant to current practice. Questions were designed to explore the level of understanding and awareness of the wider professional agenda. The interviews and questionnaires were analysed in order to ascertain common issues for participants.

2. Learning-set meetings
In order to identify key areas for development, participants were led to reflect on the core values related to teaching and learning which underpinned their professional practice. The model used to facilitate discussion was the work of Glaser (1990) who expanded Kolb's learning model by showing how a cycle (single loop theory) could be used to underpin the design and facilitation of a process of change. Thus participants explored and redefined their philosophy through critical reflection and self-awareness, examining the following areas:

■ The reality of their working environment in relation to their values and philosophy, identifying the barriers which prevented the realisation of their philosophy.

■ The ways in which these barriers might be overcome through effective management and leadership techniques.

Time was allocated at the beginning of learning-set meetings to allow participants to talk about the progress being made within their roles and introduce the themes raised. This acted not only to introduce common themes but served to prepare participants for more specific discussions further into the session. These discussions were in greater depth and explored the detail and origins of the issues identified. To support this exploration the lead coach delivered a short presentation of the theoretical principles underpinning practice related to each issue. The theory was used to introduce an academic basis for adopting a broader approach to resolving the issues raised.

Participants were left to discuss the issues, offer practical solutions and consider the ways in which the theory may be applied in the practical setting. This is the critical phase as prior to the introduction of theory and research, participants had limited exposure to theoretical perspectives on management and leadership. By becoming familiar with the specific theory and considering a practical application the likelihood of developing a broader solution-led approach is significantly enhanced. Additionally, the whole process fostered open and collaborative communication.

3. An inquiry task

The final phase involved the participants undertaking small-scale inquiries into their own practice, adopting the new peer-coaching model to support these inquiries. This phase served to offer a platform for exploring pragmatic and dynamic solutions. Once a foundation for identifying solutions had been laid, participants were in a position to guide the learning of their colleagues in a positive manner. This phase also served to draw out the characteristics of peer coaching.

Outcomes

Peer coaches

Feedback from the participants regarding the learning-set discussions was very positive. Participants welcomed the opportunity to discuss issues and stated that this was the most beneficial part of the process, claimed that it had an effective influence on their practice and raised questions about the professional development offered by heads of department to support the deputy heads in their role. This is a key finding which has many implications. There is a need to develop the communication between heads of department and the deputy heads, but also there is the need for a peer-coaching group of this kind to meet, to network and find solutions specific to their roles.

Mixed views were expressed about the theoretical input and only one participant was able to apply theoretical ideas to an actual strategy to implement change. Although this input was perceived to be interesting, it was felt that more time was needed to develop strategies that took account of these theoretical ideas.

The participants identified a number of perceived barriers to implementing a peer-coaching model in the future. Some of the perceptions raised at regular intervals by the participants were:

1. a variance in willingness to invest time;
2. contextual differences across departments;
3. a variance in leadership and modelling of desired behaviours;
4. a variance in commitment to professional development;
5. feelings of isolation.

This finding could be used to develop a shared vision with middle leaders and other staff in order to enhance the quality of teacher delivery and have a positive impact on the quality of learning. As a consequence of the experience of the peer-coaching process, two of the participants subsequently enrolled in an effective practitioners' course run by the local authority which carries master's level accreditation.

Lead coach

The benefits of undertaking this inquiry have been transformative for all concerned. The lead coach gained a great deal of personal satisfaction from having a positive impact on the development of colleagues. He derived satisfaction from initiating meetings and ensuring a clear direction for discussions in order to facilitate development. This satisfaction was most evident in the way he adapted the discussion-based approach of the learning-set meeting. He identified that in early meetings participants' reflection was not sufficiently critical and responded to this in subsequent meetings to allow participants to develop more critical reflection. As the peer-coaching process was developed and refined, it became apparent that after two learning-set meetings and two face-to-face interviews it was having the desired effect as the depth of knowledge, understanding and application of theoretical models was articulated and argued with greater coherence. The lead coach acknowledged the strength of the collaboration within the peer-coaching group as a key factor in this success. The only drawback was that the lead coach found the whole process time consuming and concluded that any school wishing to adopt a similar peer-coaching strategy in school would need to ensure that institutional support structures are put in place.

Inquiry 3

This inquiry asks 'Could the implementation of a mentoring programme for the senior leadership team facilitate professional development for both individual and institutional roles?'

Context

This inquiry is designed to ascertain whether or not there is a desire or need for a mentoring/coaching programme for members of a senior leadership team (SLT) within an urban secondary school. It also aims to identify whether or not any such programme could address the personal and professional developmental needs of the team.

In the last 30 years the mentoring of teachers has become more explicit in the work of schools with the emphasis being placed on those training to become teachers or those who are in their first year of teaching. Such mentoring is often provided by external agencies such as local authorities, providers of initial teacher training or via internal school-based programmes offering both professional and subject development. Advanced Skills Teachers (ASTs) are also expected to contribute to this area of work within a school. But interestingly, only one website for ASTs includes mentoring as an aspect of the role, stating that ASTs should act as mentors and coaches to a range of staff. Once teachers move into middle management roles any mentoring or coaching that takes place is sporadic and context dependent. Progression to senior leadership in a school (assistant headteacher, deputy headteacher or headteacher) involves a move away from mentoring into coaching through leadership routes organised by the National College for Leadership of Schools and Children's Services to fulfil the requirements of NPQH (National Professional Qualification for Headship).

The rationale for this inquiry arises from the inquirer's experience, which has identified the considerable benefits of mentoring for those entering the profession. This led the inquirer to consider whether the SLT would welcome the opportunity to be mentored. The timing of this inquiry coincided with a change of headteacher, providing a good opportunity to explore the idea with the SLT.

The SLT consists of 12 members: one headteacher, three deputy headteachers, six assistant headteachers and two co-ordinators. Some have been in post for a number of years; others have only recently taken up their current senior leadership roles (including the headteacher) so there is a variety of age and experience amongst the team members. In terms of gender balance, seven of the team are female and five are male, which may have an impact on the way in which they respond to questions about the issue. Given that many of the team have been in post for some years their perceptions of mentoring may be outdated.

In carrying out this inquiry, the inquirer has drawn on the work of writers such as Megginson and Clutterbuck (2005), Koshy (2005) and Brockbank and McGill (2006), cited earlier in the book. Additional theoretical perspectives are provided below from Wilson (2007), Foster-Turner (2006), Claxton (2002) and Law *et al.* (2007).

Wilson (2007: 15) acknowledges that, 'In modern business the practice of delivering mentoring in a coaching style is on the increase'. The blending together of the two roles reflects the changing contexts, both cultural and institutional, that mentors find themselves working in. She also identifies the 'tension' between individual and institution. Foster-Turner's (2006) book on mentoring and coaching within health and social care talks of developing the right environment for learning and highlights the idea of 'ownership' of learning opportunities:

> Developing the right environments for learning ... is crucial in order to enable effective learning to occur through whatever mode, and also for it to be directed specifically as needed by the

protagonists, their organisation, and stakeholders, especially service end-users.

(Ibid.: 7)

She concludes, 'it seems that leaders in public sector organisations, alongside their private sector colleagues have decided that coaching and mentoring is a realistic method for taking learning forward' (ibid.: 9) Closely connected to this notion of learner ownership are the ideas presented by Guy Claxton (2002) who uses the metaphor of a 'palette', and identifies four key qualities needed to maximise learning power for the individual learner. These are resilience, resourcefulness, reflection and reciprocity. There is a huge overlap between these qualities and those of mentoring. Law *et al.* (2007) propose the idea of a Universal Integrated Framework (UIF). They offer the following description of their framework:

The framework is like an onion with many layers: self, social, cultural and professional. The core of the framework, self and self-development, is grounded in a dynamic coaching/mentoring/ learning model ... it is consistent with the psychology of learning where coachees/mentees, and coaches/mentors are all learners within the process.

(Ibid.: 108)

This encapsulates the idea that learning in the coaching/mentoring relationship is reciprocal and developmental.

Process

'Action Research for Improving Practice' (Koshy 2005) has proved invaluable in shaping this inquiry. Qualitative and quantitative data were needed to assess the SLT's understanding of the issue and eliciting what they do or do not want. 'The use of questionnaires within a qualitative study often provides ideas for further exploration' (ibid.: 86). Koshy's practical advice on the advantages and disadvantages of using different methods of collecting data influenced the questionnaire designed for this investigation so that it used a combination of open and closed questions to provide a tight focus on the understanding of mentoring by the respondents and yet allowed them to relate their own experience and ideas.

In order to carry out the inquiry the headteacher's permission was sought to address the SLT at one of their meetings. At this meeting a Powerpoint presentation outlined the inquiry in order to stimulate thinking about the issue of mentoring. A questionnaire was then distributed to be completed and returned within 48 hours. The short turnaround time was deliberate as most of the questions only required a brief response and the responses needed to be as open as possible, a snapshot of their thoughts and opinions at that moment.

The first 10 questions gathered information about their perceptions and experiences of mentoring. It was intriguing to see whether the initial thoughts and experiences expressed about the way 'mentoring' moves into 'coaching' as peoples' careers progress were borne out by the questionnaire responses. The last question was more open, allowing for respondents to outline their 'ideal' thoughts. The similarities and differences in their responses yielded both quantitative and qualitative data for analysis and interpretation.

Once their responses were collated, four members of the team were chosen to interview – the headteacher, a deputy headteacher and two assistant headteachers. The interviewees were selected from the responses they had made to the final (open) question and to ensure representation of the different sub-groups of the SLT. Finally, some recommendations were formulated for the SLT to consider alongside the other findings.

Outcomes

The findings from the questionnaire can be summarised in three ways:

1. the responses that dealt with definitions of mentoring;
2. the responses that dealt with the process of mentoring;
3. the responses to a potential mentoring programme or framework.

1. Definitions of mentoring
These responses identified a strong commitment to the idea of personal development for the mentee reflecting the idea of a personal journey running alongside the professional and the need for

professional development opportunities which will address both. The choice of language used by the respondents revealed an outdated understanding of mentoring which is based on the traditional model of an older, more experienced person 'imparting wisdom' to a younger, less experienced person. The older, more experienced colleagues felt that mentoring is something they do for others rather than something they receive. The questionnaires also confirmed a perception that once people have moved into senior management positions 'mentoring' stops and 'coaching' becomes the nearest thing to replace it. Many expressed a desire to know more about each other's roles and to take more of a team approach to their work. The inquirer realised there was a need to update knowledge of mentoring and coaching definitions and models to broaden their thinking about what they feel is most appropriate for them as a team.

2. Process of mentoring

Here the responses showed a mixed picture of what mentoring had been received and what they would like to see as part of any programme for themselves. What did emerge strongly was the notion of 'formal' and 'informal' mentoring. Their idea of 'formal' mentoring seemed to be a situation where someone is identified as a mentor and structured, regular meetings occur. 'Informal' mentoring was described by the respondents as a mentee self-selecting a mentor and encounters taking place in a less structured and more opportunistic way. It is the view of this inquirer that these responses can be matched with Brockbank and McGill's (2006: 11) map of mentoring and coaching approaches as 'functionalist' (formal) and 'engagement (informal) approaches.

Formal (functionalist) mentoring would address the needs of the institution by giving objectivity to any mentoring activities/feedback. Informal (engagement) mentoring would meet the individual's needs. However, according to Brockbank and McGill (2006), both these approaches sustain current practice or equilibrium rather than bringing about change or transformation. The inquirer concluded that it would be useful to give the SLT the opportunity to examine Brockbank and McGill's (2006) ideas about 'evolutionary mentoring' (p. 14) to show how transformation could be motivated. Respondents made it clear that they valued the personal approaches which allow face-to-face interaction and spontaneous exchanges. A number of respondents used the words 'supportive' when describing the kind of processes they wanted and valued. This would suggest that an 'informal' mentoring is wanted alongside clear tasks which focus on specific aspects of professional skills.

3. Frameworks or programmes for mentoring

These responses showed very clearly that there is a strong desire to have a system of mentoring for the SLT which covers the full spectrum of informal and formal mentoring. They also wanted something that would address both the needs of the individual and the institution, the personal as well as the professional. Their responses to the questionnaires included suggestions related to the purposes, structure and content of such a system of mentoring.

The purposes identified included the following:

- to maintain a balance between individuals' needs and school roles;
- to understand the roles of other members of SLT;
- the empowerment of the individual;
- to establish protocols/procedures to facilitate 'learning conversations';
- to improve the effectiveness of individuals and the team.

The inquirer linked these purposes to the principle of both mentor and mentees being seen as *learners*, which draws on Claxton's (2002) framework to develop learning power and the UIF of Law *et al.* (2007).

The respondents wanted the system to include:

- a chance to reflect on the purpose of SLT as a collective experience;
- genuine choice of PMP (Performance Management Process) leader;
- to be assigned an external mentor;
- regular feedback;
- tasks focused on professional skills;
- aspects of life coaching.

In order to gain ownership of the mentoring system the respondents wanted to change the school's current system of performance management breaking away from the traditional hierarchical allocation of PMP leader. The inquirer identified a tension between the desire for life coaching and the focus on professional skills.

There were four significant questions raised by respondents when considering the development of a mentoring system:

- Does it have to be compulsory?
- Who would deliver such a programme?
- Who needs what kind of mentoring and how would that be ascertained?
- What would be covered in the programme?

These questions confirmed the concerns about ownership and empowerment. However, such questions also show a willingness to reflect on and revisit the values that underpin the purpose of the SLT. This in turn may help the SLT to define for themselves their purpose and the values they wish to put at the heart of any devised system.

For the interview four respondents were selected to reflect the range of responses to the final open-ended question in the questionnaire and to ensure representation from the major sub-groups within the SLT.

Interviewee 1 wanted a formal programme consisting of termly meetings and regular email contact with an external mentor who would be assigned to the mentee. This respondent wanted the programme to address personal as well as professional development but wanted an emphasis on the development of professional skills.

Interviewee 2 wanted to open up 'learning horizons' which used practical tasks as well as discussions. This respondent suggested the need for open, detailed, reflective discussion which reconsidered the purpose of the SLT. A reallocation of professional development time was also suggested to facilitate discussion along with a move away from current performance management practices.

Interviewee 3 felt that the time was right to start 'linking' members of the SLT not only within the school but with outside partners too. This respondent also acknowledged the importance of regular feedback from such partnerships to bring about 'truly reflective practice'.

Interviewee 4 wanted to develop a coaching rather than a mentoring system as mentoring was deemed too hierarchical. The respondent proposed a system where someone is 'empowering the individual to arrive at their own solutions' through reflective talk and using feedback from observations.

Recommendations

The following recommendations arising from the inquiry can be linked to the work of Claxton (2002). The inquirer considers his four key 'learning dispositions' of resourcefulness, resilience, reciprocity and reflectiveness (ibid.) as fundamental to a healthy mentoring relationship and fit well with the reported ideas from the SLT. The recommendations of the inquirer are as follows:

■ Revisit the values that underpin the institution.
■ Update the SLT's knowledge and understanding of mentoring and coaching.
■ Introduce a mentoring programme for the SLT that is pragmatic and fits the ethos of the institution as well as individual personal and professional need (this should include a range of mentoring and coaching strategies, e.g. co-coaching and specialist coaching).
■ Explore the possibilities of using external mentors to provide an opportunity for objective feedback and sharing the experience of other institutions.
■ Use the ASTs as critical inquirers with access to other institutions and networks to help turn ideas into action and evaluate proposals and decisions.

* * *

These three inquiries illustrate the eight elements of the practitioner inquiry spectrum identified in Chapter 4. All three inquiries demonstrate collaborations with a range of teachers, to identify reciprocal professional learning at different levels. They all take a critical look at aspects of mentoring and coaching practice in the schools. All three inquiries enable the participants to act as agents of change within their schools through a process of critical inquiry. Different types of evidence are collected and examined and the interpretations of findings from the inquiries trigger transformation of both individual and institutional professional learning and practices. Dissemination of these findings is an important aspect of the process of transformation and the impact of all three inquiries within the school is evident. In each inquiry the potential also exists for more public dissemination of this impact in professional contexts beyond the individual institution.

Investigation for Chapter 8

Purpose

To construct an inquiry focused on setting up a new mentoring and/or coaching process. This process should involve a group or team of professionals within the school and explore the use of wider mentoring and/or coaching collaborations within the school context. The inquiry will have the potential for whole-school impact.

Action

1. Read the examples of inquiries in this chapter to inform this investigation.
2. Select a suitable group or team which would benefit from a new or changed mentoring and/or coaching process. This group or team may be from already established mentoring and/or coaching relationships or you may wish to set up a new collaboration or introduce an aspect of mentoring and/or coaching to an established team.
3. Discuss and agree with the team a focus for the inquiry which relates to the development of a new mentoring and/or coaching process. This process aims to use mentoring and/or coaching collaborations for professional learning for the team. Ensure that the process which is agreed is manageable within the time and resource limits available.
4. Agree the structure and modes of communication for the collaboration (e.g. frequency and timings of meetings, face-to-face or electronic communication).
5. Decide on the evidence required for the inquiry which will assess the effectiveness of the mentoring and/or coaching process developed. Decide on the data required to provide this evidence. The evidence could include the following:

   - notes from interviews and meetings;
   - responses to questionnaires;
   - summaries of documentary evidence;
   - diary notes;
   - notes from observations of practice;
   - audio or video recording and photographs.

6. Develop a schedule for the inquiry which will allow for appropriate evidence to be collected which assesses the success of the process implemented. Use the inquiries in chapter eight as a guide for developing a schedule.
7. Ensure that ethical guidelines are followed. Those published by the British Educational Research Association (www.bera.ac.uk) are a useful source of information. In summary, consideration must be given to the following:

   ■ obtaining permission from participants;
   ■ explaining the purpose of the inquiry;
   ■ ensuring anonymity of participants;
   ■ sharing information collected with participants for verification;
   ■ being non-intrusive;
   ■ ensuring secure storage of data.

8. Collect the data in line with these guidelines.
9. Analyse the data in order to assess the effectiveness of the new mentoring and/or coaching process set up by the inquiry.
10. Discuss this analysis with the team involved in the mentoring and/or coaching process to identify issues and recommendations. Disseminate these as appropriate within and beyond the school context.

Evaluation of the inquiry

Use Evaluation Templates 1.1 and 1.2 on pp. 13–14 to assess the scale of impact of the collaborative mentoring- and/or coaching-focused inquiry on professional learning for the individual, the institution and the education profession.

9

A new perspective: mentoring and coaching as collaborative professional inquiry

This chapter concludes the book by clarifying the new perspective on mentoring and coaching for school contexts which has been progressively constructed in previous chapters. It is a perspective which builds on a range of conceptions and current uses of mentoring and coaching designed to develop supportive professional learning relationships. However, this new perspective proposes a model of collaboration for these mentoring and coaching relationships which is centred on a focused process of critical inquiry and which has the potential to provide professional learning which is both transformative and empowering for teachers.

The key theoretical ideas identified in Part I which contribute to this new perspective on mentoring and coaching in schools relate to:

- professional learning (Kolb 1984, Marsick and Watkins 1990, Watkins *et al.* 2002, Brockbank and McGill 2006) and knowledge (Popper 1972, Laurillard 1993);
- practitioner inquiry (Elliott 1991, Kemmis and McTaggart 2005, Reason and Bradbury 2001, Zeichner 2003, O'Leary 2004, Nelson 2005, Groundwater-Smith and Mockler 2006, Fook 2010, Campbell and McNamara 2010);
- collaboration and co-construction (Bohm 1996, Boud 2010, Livingston and Shiach 2010);
- metaphorical representations of the context for all of these (Bhabha 1994, Smith 2000, Ponte 2007 and 2010, Hulme and Cracknell 2010).

These key ideas form the conceptual basis for implementing teacher inquiries within mentoring and coaching collaborations. Examples of such inquiries are presented in Part II. These inquiries demonstrate not only the uses of mentoring and coaching relationships to carry out practitioner inquiry but also explore the nature, purpose, quality and organisation of mentoring and coaching in schools.

A mentoring and coaching relationship can assess whether it is adopting a successful practitioner inquiry approach to professional learning if it addresses the principles which were identified in Chapters 3 and 4 and summarised below:

- achieving coherence between theoretical, personal and professional knowledge and experience;
- enabling teachers with a range of knowledge and experience to engage in dialogue and collaborative reflection;
- developing the co-construction of new professional knowledge;
- using the mentoring and coaching relationship as a platform where shared goals and principles are continuously reviewed and contested;
- understanding how critical inquiry enhances professional learning;
- viewing critical inquiry as both a useful learning process and an ongoing 'state of mind'.

These theoretical concepts and principles come together to produce the radically new perspective on mentoring and coaching in schools proposed throughout the book. For schools and teachers this new perspective offers a range of advantages for the enhancement of both individual and institutional professional learning within mentoring and coaching relationships. These advantages will be experienced to different degrees according to the nature and the scale of the practitioner inquiry, as discussed in Chapter 4. Throughout this book, teachers have been given practical ideas on exploring these theoretical concepts and principles in order to understand and experience the advantages of this new perspective. Some of these advantages are:

- Reciprocal transformative professional learning that does not rely on institutional hierarchies of role and status.
- Teachers have ownership of the questioning process and learning

outcomes as well as investment in creating and examining the focus for the inquiry.

- The processes and outcomes are transparent and outward looking allowing for impact beyond the specific mentoring and coaching relationship to the wider institution.
- Provision of a professional focus to a relationship which could otherwise become unstructured and inward looking whilst still addressing affective factors pertinent to the learning.
- The process does not necessarily require a substantial additional investment of resources.

Mentoring and coaching relationships provide the collaborative context for a powerful process of professional learning inquiry which has the potential for dynamic, wide-scale transformation of professional practice throughout the teaching profession.

Bibliography

Adey, P., Hewitt, G., Hewitt, J. and Landau, N. (2004) *The Professional Development of Teachers: Practice and Theory*. Dordrecht: Kluwer Academic.

Argyris, C. and Schon, D. (1996) *Organisational Learning II: Theory, Method and Practice*. Wokingham: Addison-Wesley.

Arthur, J., Davison, J. and Moss, J. (1997) *Subject Mentoring in the Secondary School*. London: Routledge.

Askew, S. C. (2006) *Coaching and Mentoring in Higher Education: A Learning Centered Approach*. London: Institute of Education.

Belenky, M. F., Clinchy, B. M., Goldberger, N. R. and Tarule, J. M. (1986) *Women's Ways of Knowing: the Development of Self, Voice and Mind*. New York: Basic Books.

BERA (British Educational Research Association) (2004) *Revised Ethical Guidelines for Educational Research*. Retrieved April 2010, from www.bera.ac.uk/publications/guides.php.

Bhabha, H. (1994) *The Location of Culture*. London: Routledge.

Blackmore, J. (2002) 'Is it only "what works" that counts on new knowledge economies? Evidence-based practice, educational research and teacher education in Australia', paper presented to the 'Changing Futures' conference, University of New England, Armidale, February 2002.

Bohm, D. (1996) *On Dialogue*. Routledge: London.

Boud, D. (2010) 'Relocating reflection in the context of practice', in S. Kilminster, M. Zukas, H. Bradbury and N. Frost (eds) *Beyond Reflective Practice: New Approaches to Professional Lifelong Learning*. Abingdon: Routledge.

Boud, D., Cohen, R. and Walker, D. (1993) *Using Experience for Learning*. Bristol: Open University Press.

Brockbank, A. and McGill, I. (2006) *Facilitating Reflective Learning Through Mentoring and Coaching*. London: Kogan Page.

Bruner, J. (1986) *Actual Minds, Possible Worlds*. Cambridge, MA: Harvard University Press.

Campbell, A. (2007) *Practitioner Research*. London: TLRP. Online at http://www.tlrp.org/capacity/rm/wt/campbell (accessed 20 Dec 2010).

Campbell, A. and McNamara, O. (2010) 'Mapping the field of practitioner research, inquiry and professional learning in educational contexts: a review', in A. Campbell and S. Groundwater-Smith (eds) *Connecting Inquiry and Professional Learning in Education*. Abingdon: Routledge.

Carnell, E. and Lodge, C. (2002) *Supporting Effective Learning*. London: Sage.

Carnell, E., MacDonald, J. and Askew, S. (2006) *Coaching and Mentoring in Higher Education: A Learning-Centred Approach*. London: Institute of Education, University of London.

Carr, W. and Kemmis, S. (1986) *Becoming Critical: Education, Knowledge and Action Research*. London: Falmer.

Claxton, G. (2002) *Building Learning Power*. Bristol: TLO.

Clinchy, B. M. (1996) 'Connected and separate knowing: towards a marriage of two minds', in N. R. Goldberger, J. M. Tarule, B. M. Clinchy and M. F. Belenky (eds) *Knowledge, Difference and Power: Essays Inspired by Women's Ways of Knowing*. New York: Basic Books.

Clutterbuck, D. (1998) *Learning Alliances: Tapping into Talent*. London: Chartered Institute of Personnel and Development.

Clutterbuck, D. (2003) *The Problem with Research in Mentoring*. The Coaching and Mentoring Network, Clutterbuck Associates. Online at www.coachingnetwork.org.uk/resourcecentre/articles/ViewArticle.asp?artId=82 (accessed 17 Feb 2011).

Clutterbuck, D. and. Ragins, B. R. (2002) *Mentoring and Diversity: An International Perspective*. Oxford: Butterworth-Heinemann.

Cochran-Smith, M. and Lytle, S. I. (1993) *Inside Outside: Teacher Research and Knowledge*. New York: Teachers College Press.

Cohen, L. and Mannion, L. (1994) *Research Methods in Education*. London: Routledge.

Colley, H. (2003) *Mentoring for Social Inclusion: A Critical Approach to Nurturing Mentor Relationships*. London: Routledge/Falmer.

Connor, M. and Pokora, J. (2007) *Coaching and Mentoring at Work: Principles for Effective Practice*. Buckingham: Open University Press.

Cordingley, P., Bell, M., Rundell, B. and Evans, D. (2003) 'The impact of collaborative CPD on classroom teaching and learning', in *Research Evidence in Education Library*. London: EPPI-Centre, Social Science Research Unit, Institute of Education, University of London.

Cranton, P. (1996) *Professional Development as Transformative Learning*. San Francisco, CA: Jossey-Bass.

CUREE (Centre for the Use of Research Evidence in Education) (2004–5) *Mentoring and Coaching for Learning: Summary Report of the Mentoring and Coaching CPD Capacity Building Project*. Coventry: CUREE.

DCSF (Department for Children, Schools and Families) (2005) *National Framework for Mentoring and Coaching*. London: DCSF.

DCSF (2008) *Statutory Guidance on the Induction Period for Newly Qualified Teachers (NQTs) in England*. London: DCSF.

Denscombe, M. (1998) *Good Research Guide for Small-Scale Social Research Projects*. Buckingham: Open University Press.

Dewey (1938) *Experience and Education*. New York: Touchstone: Simon & Schuster (first Touchstone edition published 1997).

DfE (Department for Education) (1992) *Initial Teacher Training (Secondary Phase) Circular 9/92*. London: DfE.

Dietz, M. E. (1998) *Responses as Frameworks for Change*. Victoria: Hawker Brownlow Education.

Downey, M. (1999) *Effective Coaching*. London: Orion Business Books.

DuFour, R., Eaker, R. and Many, T. (2006). *Learning by Doing: A Handbook for Professional Learning Communities at Work*. Bloomington, IN: Solution Tree.

Ebbutt, D. (1985) 'Educational action research: some general concerns and specific quibbles', in R. Burgess (ed.) *Issues in Educational Research: Qualitative Methods*. Lewes: Falmer.

Egan, G. (1990) *The Skilled Helper: A Systematic Approach to Effective Helping*, 4th edn. Pacific Grove, CA: Brooks/Cole.

Egan, G. (2002) *The Skilled Helper: A Problem Management Approach and Opportunity Approach to Helping*. Pacific Grove, CA: Brooks/Cole.

Elliott, J. (1991) *Action Research for Educational Change*. Buckingham: Open University Press.

Fletcher, S. (2000) *Mentoring in Schools: A Handbook of Good Practice*. London: Kogan Page.

Fook, J. (2010) 'Beyond reflective practice: reworking the "critical", in critical reflection', in H. Bradbury, N. Frost, S. Kilminster, S. and M. Zukas (eds) *Beyond Reflective Practice: New Approaches to Professional Lifelong Learning*. Abingdon: Routledge.

Foster-Turner, J. (2006) *Coaching and Mentoring in Health and Social Care: The Essential Manual for Professionals and Organisations*. Oxford: Radcliffe.

Furlong, J. and Maynard, T. (1995) *Mentoring Student Teachers: The Growth of Professional Knowledge*. London: Routledge.

Gardener, H. (1983) *Frames of Mind: The Theory of Multiple Intelligences*. New York: Basic Books.

Garvey, R., Stokes, P. and Megginson, D. (2009) *Coaching and Mentoring: Theory and Practice*. London: Sage.

Glaser, R. (1990) *Designing and Facilitating Adult Learning*. King of Prussia, Pennsylvania: Organisation, Design and Development Inc. HRDQ.

Goleman, D. (1995) *Emotional Intelligence: Why It Can Matter More Than IQ*. New York: Bantam Books.

Groundwater-Smith, S. and Mockler, N. (2006) 'Research that counts: practitioner research and the academy', in *Counterpoints on the Quality and*

Impact of Educational Research. Special Edition of *Review of Australian Research in Education,* Number 6.

Hagger, H. B., Burn, K. and McIntyre, D. (1993) *The School Mentor Handbook: Essential Skills and Strategies for Working with Student Teachers.* London: Kogan Page.

Hopkins, D. (2002) *A Teacher's Guide to Classroom Research,* 3rd edn. Buckingham: Open University Press.

Hulme, R. and Cracknell. D. (2010) 'Learning across boundaries: developing trans-professional understanding through practitioner inquiry', in A. Campbell and S. Groundwater-Smith (eds) *Connecting Inquiry and Professional Learning in Education: International Perspectives and Practical Solutions.* Abingdon: Routledge.

Jaworski, B. (2006) 'Theory and practice in mathematics teaching development: critical inquiry as a mode of learning in teaching', *Journal of Mathematics Teacher Education,* 9, 187–211.

Joyce, B. and Showers, B. (2002) *Student Achievement Through Staff Development,* 3rd edn. London: Longman.

Kemmis, S. and McTaggart, R. (2005) 'Participatory action research: communicative action and the public sphere', in N. K. Denzin and Y. S. Lincoln (eds) *The Sage Handbook of Qualitative Research,* 3rd edn. London: Sage.

Kilminster, S., Zukas, M., Bradbury, H. and Frost, N. (2010) 'Introduction and overview', in H. Bradbury, N. Frost, S. Kilminster and M. Zukas (eds) *Beyond Reflective Practice: New Approaches to Professional Lifelong Learning.* Abingdon: Routledge.

Knowles, M. S. (1980) *The Modern Practice of Adult Education: From Pedagogy to Andragogy,* 2nd edn. New York: Cambridge Books.

Kolb, D. (1984) *Experiential Learning: Experience as the Source of Learning and Development.* Englewood Cliffs, NJ: Prentice Hall.

Koshy, V. (2005) *Action Research for Improving Practice: A Practical Guide.* London: Sage.

Laurillard, D. (1993) *Rethinking University Teaching: A Framework for the Effective Use of Educational Technology.* London: Routledge.

Law, H., Ireland, S. and Hussain, Z. (2007) *The Psychology of Coaching, Mentoring and Learning.* Chichester: John Wiley.

Lingard, B. and Renshaw, P. (2010) 'Teaching as a research-informed and research-informing profession', in A. Campbell and S. Groundwater-Smith (eds) *Connecting Inquiry and Professional Learning in Education: International Perspectives and Practical Solutions.* Abingdon: Routledge.

Livingston, K. and Shiach, L. (2010) 'Co-constructing a new model of teacher education', in A. Campbell and S. Groundwater-Smith (eds) *Connecting Inquiry and Professional Learning in Education: International Perspectives and Practical Solutions.* Abingdon: Routledge.

Marsick, V. J. and Watkins, K. E. (1990) *Informal and Incidental Learning in the Workplace.* London: Routledge.

Maynard, T. (1997) *An Introduction to Primary Mentoring*. London: Cassell.

Megginson, D. and Clutterbuck, D. (2005) *Techniques for Coaching and Mentoring*. Oxford: Elsevier Butterworth-Heinemann.

Mezirow, J. (1994) 'Understanding transformation theory', *Adult Education Quarterly*, 44, 222–32.

NCLSCS (National College for Leadership of Schools and Children's Services) (2010) 'About the National College', www.nationalcollege.org.uk/index/about-us (accessed 21 Feb 2010).

Nelson, T. H. (2005) 'Knowledge interactions in teacher–scientist partnerships: negotiation, consultation and rejection', *Journal of Teacher Education*, 56(4), 382–95.

O'Leary, Z. (2004) *The Essential Guide to Doing Research*. London: Sage.

Ponte, P. (2007) 'Postgraduate education as platform: a conceptualisation', in J. Van Swet, P. Ponte and B. Smit (eds) *Postgraduate Programs as Platform: a Research-Led Approach*. Rotterdam: Sense Publishers.

Ponte, P. (2010) 'Postgraduate programmes as platforms: coming together and doing research for a common moral purpose', in A. Campbell and S. Groundwater-Smith (eds) *Connecting Inquiry and Professional Learning in Education: International Perspectives and Practical Solutions*. Abingdon: Routledge.

Popper, K. R. (1972) *Objective Knowledge: An Evolutionary Approach*. Oxford: Clarendon Press.

Punter, A. (2007) *Mentor Development for Teacher Training: A Scenario-Based Approach*. University of Hertfordshire Press.

Ragins, B. R. and Kram, K. E. (2007) *The Handbook of Mentoring at Work: Theory, Research and Practice*. London: Sage.

Reason, P. and Bradbury, H. (2001) *Handbook of Action Research: Participative Inquiry and Practice*. London: Sage.

Rhodes, C. S. (2004) *A Practical Guide to Mentoring, Coaching and Peer Networking*. London: Falmer.

Rogers, J. (2004) *Coaching Skills: A Handbook*. Maidenhead: Open University Press.

Schon, D. (1983) *The Reflective Practitioner: How Professionals Think in Action*. New York: Basic Books.

Slavit, D. and Nelson, T. H. (2009) 'Supported collaborative teacher inquiry', in D. Slavit, T. H. Nelson and A. Kennedy (eds) *Perspectives on Supported Collaborative Teacher Inquiry*. Abingdon: Routledge.

Smith, R. (2000) 'The future of teacher education: principles and prospects', *Asia Pacific Journal of Teacher Education*, 28(1), 7–28.

Stenhouse, L. (1975) *An Introduction to Curriculum Research and Development*. London: Heinemann.

Stephens, P. (1996) *Essential Mentoring Skills: A Practical Handbook for School-Based Educators*. Cheltenham: Stanley Thornes.

TDA (Training and Development Agency for Schools) (2008) *Professional*

Standards for Qualified Teacher Status and Requirements for Initial Teacher Training (Revised 2008). London: TDA.

TDA (2009a) *Guidance to Accompany the Professional Standards for Qualified Teacher Status and Requirements for Initial Teacher Training (Revised 2008)*. London: TDA.

TDA (2009b) Masters in Teaching and Learning Coaching Strategy, V1.0 18, November.

TDA (2009c) *Strategy for the Professional Development of the Children's Workforce in Schools 2009–12*. London: TDA.

Vygotsky, L. (1978) *Mind in Society: The Development of Higher Psychological Processes*. Cambridge MA: Harvard University Press.

Watkins, C. (2000) *Learning About Learning: Resources for Supporting Effective Learning*. London: Routledge Falmer and NAPCE School Improvement Network Research.

Watkins, C. and Whalley, C. (1993) 'Mentoring beginner teachers – issues for schools to anticipate and manage', *School Organisation*, 13(2), 129–38.

Watkins, C., Carnell, E., Lodge, C., Wagner, P. and Whalley, C. (1998) *Learning About Learning*. Coventry: NAPCE.

Watkins, C., Carnell, E., Lodge, C., Wagner, P. and Whalley, C. (2002) *Effective Learning*. National School Improvement Network. Research Matters, number 17. London: Institute of Education, University of London.

Wells, G. (1999) *Dialogic Inquiry: Towards a Sociocultural Practice and Theory of Education*. Cambridge: Cambridge University Press.

Wenger, E. (1998) *Communities of Practice*. Cambridge: Cambridge University Press.

Whitmore, J. (1996) *Coaching for Performance*. London: Nicholas Brealey.

Wilson, C. (2007) *Best Practice in Performance Coaching: A Handbook for Leaders, Coaches, HR Professionals and Organisations*. London: Kogan Page.

Zeichner, K. (2001) 'Educational Action Research', in P. Reason and H. Bradbury (eds) *Handbook of Action Research: Participative Inquiry and Practice*. London: Sage.

Zeichner, K. (2003) 'Teacher research and professional development', *Educational Action Research*, 11(2), 319.

Zeichner, K. and Noffke, S. (2001) 'Practitioner research', in V. Richardson (ed.) *Handbook of Research on Teaching*, 4th edn. Washington, DC: AERA.

Websites

www.buildinglearningpower.co.uk
www.mmc.nhs.uk (Modernising Medical Careers)

Index

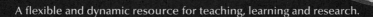